This Book

presented to the

CHURCH
LIBRARY
IN MEMORY OF

FRANK ALEXANDER
(January 1990)

BY

Mr. & Mrs. Charles Harper

Code 4386-23, No. 3, Broadman Supplies, Nashville, Tenn. Printed in USA

The Joys of Aging

Martin A. Janis

WORD PUBLISHING
Dallas · London · Sydney · Singapore

Library of Congress Cataloging in Publication Data

Janis, Martin A., 1913–
    The joys of aging / by Martin A. Janis; foreword by Norman Vincent Peale.
      p. cm.
    ISBN 0–8499–0663–6
    1. Aged—United States—Social conditions.   2. Aging—United States.   3. Self-realization.   I. Title.
HQ1064.U5J36 1988
305.2′6′0973—dc19   88-19774
                                        CIP

Printed in the United States of America

89801239 RRD 987654321

My joys of aging have been:
The years of love, understanding and encouragement
of my wife, Anne;
The enthusiasm of our daughter, Marlana;
The belief and anticipation of my grandson,
Martin Adam, in this book's completion;
The memory of our children, Jeffrey and Josephine,
who are with us in spirit;
The thousands of senior citizens who urged
me to put my words into print.

Thank You

No book is done without assistance, and this one is no exception. In addition to the individuals mentioned in my dedication, let me formally thank the following:

My good friend and author, Robert Shook, who pointed me in the right direction.

The Bonham family, Roger, Jeanne and Christopher, for their superb editorial work, research and typing.

And, not least, Dr. Norman Vincent Peale for his assurances as to the value of *The Joys of Aging* as reflected in his foreword. Thanks, too, to Dr. Peale for the inspiration of his positive-thinking philosophy which is to be found in all of his writings since the 1930s.

Contents

Foreword

The Joys of Aging by Martin A. Janis is the best book on the subject of getting older that has come my way.

The author, the Honorable Martin A. Janis, is preeminently qualified to write a book on this subject. As a member of the Cabinet of the former Ohio Governor James A. Rhodes for sixteen years, Mr. Janis established the Administration on Aging. The National Association of State Units on Aging presented its twentieth anniversary achievement award to him in recognition of his outstanding work on aging.

I'm one of those who is growing older. Come to think of it, who isn't? I'm told that there are eighty million kids in the United States. They will all get older, too, as the clock goes around. So the generations proceed.

But some of us are now what they call "elderly," or senior citizens, neither of which terms much appeals to me personally. I've just always considered myself a man named Norman Vincent Peale. It happens that I've been around for a long while. But so what? I'm still the same person. Granted, I've experienced some physical changes as do all older people, but that doesn't need to invalidate one's personality.

I had a friend named Frank Bering who came from Lynchburg, Ohio, where my people originated. Frank became part owner of three big hotels in Chicago and was still managing one of them at age 85. It happened to be one of the most popular convention hotels in the United States, and I was staying there and speaking to a convention luncheon of more than 1,000 persons. Frank was supervising the event, and I watched him with admiration.

"Frank," I said, "how old are you anyway?"

He sort of glared at me, "What's the matter? Isn't your room O.K. and the meals, too?"

"Sure are," I replied.

"Well, then, what's it matter how old I am?"

"Well," I responded, "I know how old you are anyway, for you went to school with my mother."

"Tell you something, son," he continued (and that "son" went over big with me), punching me affectionately in the chest, "live your life and forget your age."

Now, of course, forgetting your age isn't all that easy. But a positive mental attitude toward yourself can help minimize the domination of age.

We had a friend in New York named Mary Bussing, a wonderful woman of the old school. She lived to be more than 90 years of age, but carried herself always with the same old charm and vigor. She told me, "I'm so happy and interested that when I look in the mirror and see an old lady, I'm surprised, for I feel as I always did."

This book by Martin A. Janis will help every older person to continue being a person with all that personality really signifies. Moreover, it will give a new and exciting view of older people in your family, and it can help all younger people, in their time, to become wonderful old people.

Anyway, this book is replete with wisdom, down-to-earth common sense and good humor. It's very enjoyable reading. Written by one of the greatest of our authorities on aging, it will make an invaluable contribution to our immense population of older folks.

Norman Vincent Peale, D.D., LL.D.

Introduction

"Yes, the years after 65 offer new opportunity, new adventures and new joys . . . ."

This book is about a modern phenomenon: the New 65+ Generation. Never before in the history of mankind have so many individuals reached age 65, much less gone beyond it. Never before have so many been so healthy in body and mind at 65+. Never before have so many experienced the joys of aging.

According to the dictionary, a generation is "the term of years accepted as the average period between the birth of parents and the birth of their offspring."

At age 65+, many of us can look forward to an additional 20 to 30 years of life—the span of an entire generation. If put to good use, this time can be beneficial to ourselves, family, friends, and community.

In a curious way, the writing of this book was prompted by my association individually and in meetings with thousands of persons 65+ since 1965. I came to marvel at their outlook on life.

Almost every day, I heard or read of the numerous ways they were dealing with the challenge of aging. I was overwhelmed by their inventiveness, their creativity, their joy of living. Granted, there were financial problems for some, the scourge of loneliness for others, the problems brought on by disabilities for still others. But for the creative optimists, those who saw the future as brimming with opportunity, the 65+ years have become the happiest of their lives. I knew that I wanted to tell this good news to others.

So you see, in an odd way, today's seniors gave rise to this book and, in an even more curious way, helped me to write it.

As you can imagine, a great deal of thought went into deciding the approach to this book. For example:

• The number 65+ might look a little strange on the page, but it was chosen with forethought. Think of it this way: at your age you're not worth*less*—you're worth *more*—hence, 65+. The plus sign can also stand for added life.

• Certainly a dilemma for me was the term I should use to denote those over 65. No doubt you've seen them all: senior, senior citizen, oldster, older person, older American, elderly and the one I often use in this book— 65+er. The one I have not seen any reference to, but which I would like to substitute for senior citizen, is *seasoned citizen*. In practice, since this newly coined term is not universally used as yet, I have employed all the foregoing terms, choosing the one that seemed the most appropriate within the context of the writing. To stick to just one term, my editors and I felt, would become monotonous; variety added interest to the writing. (However, I'm still partial to seasoned citizen and perhaps should lead a national crusade for its adoption.)

• The book was to be inspirational as well as informative and instructive. If sometimes the book seems ministerial in its tone, it is meant to be; for I have never had qualms about injecting God and religion into my thoughts and advice on growing older in a satisfying, fulfilling, and happy fashion.

In essence, this book is about the art of living. Therefore, I hope that it will also interest persons under 65 and be a reminder that to reach 65 is a privilege denied to many, and that there is a great life to be lived after 65.

In this book you will read a lot less about seniors as a group than you will as individuals, although in an early chapter we'll take a look at seniors in some depth as we define the New 65+ Generation. Then we'll set that profile aside and think of you, the 65+er, as an individual, different from any other on earth.

Regrettably, in our new technological society, the individual has become lost. Yet, how important are the experiences of life itself, the values that make life worthwhile, the living by the Golden Rule, so that our lives do matter and mean something to others.

We who are of the New 65+ Generation can be reminders of the importance of the individual by the example of our actions. Individually, we influence those around us by our actions. Collectively, think of the impact we make on society.

Does that sound far-fetched? Just recall the closing ceremony of the 1984 Summer Olympics held in Los Angeles. The most moving and impressive part of that ceremony came when those in attendance were asked to join hands while the song, "To Touch Someone," was being sung. Simultaneously, all over the world, people watching were also holding hands and singing. What a memorable scene and what a reminder that we need each other.

Looking back on my more than twenty years of meeting with multitudes of persons 65+, I can attest that the majority reflect the philosophy so movingly presented at the closing ceremony of the Olympics. To make those last years of the New Generation meaningful, to feel that your life made a difference, that those with whom you had associated were a little better because of your presence, is a worthy goal. Each of us is an individual and we are all brothers and sisters.

Yes, the years after 65 offer new opportunity—new adventures and new joys in what can be the most rewarding and fulfilling period of your life.

With this book I offer you signposts and suggestions for your continuing journey. As actor Mickey Rooney once said in benediction to an audience of seniors: "Have a happy life!"

1

Life Begins at 65

A Great Time to Be Alive

---

*". . . life doesn't begin at 40 at all—
it really begins at 65."*

At the top of the nonfiction best-seller list in America in 1933 was a book entitled *Life Begins at Forty* by Walter Pitkin,[1] a professor of journalism at Columbia University. At that time, middle age was considered to be between the ages of 35 and 50. Today, biomedical scientists define middle age as 50 to 70, and so, by comparison, life doesn't begin at 40 at all—it really begins at 65.

For the first time in the history of mankind, 65 does not mean the end—it means new opportunities. As newspapers and magazines tell us, advances in medicine, public health and work conditions have contributed to an increase in the number of persons reaching 65. Today, one out of every eight Americans is 65 or older.

True, there are some 65+ who are not able to enjoy those extra years by reason of poor health or meager financial resources, but they are the exception rather than the rule. For the majority of us who are 65+, as the insurance actuarial tables reveal, we can anticipate an additional 15 or 20 years of good health and active life.

Carl's Story

But, understandably, many who reach retirement refuse to let go of their working life. When Carl retired at 65, his co-workers and friends held a party for him and presented him and his wife with tickets for a cruise. Perhaps that should have given him a hint of how they felt and what was in store for him.

The day after the party, Carl slept late, had a second cup of coffee, and took his time reading the morning newspaper. "This is the life," he said to his wife, who was delighted at first to have him home. Then Carl found it was a problem to fill his afternoons.

"Say, honey, I have an idea. Let's go on that cruise!" Carl exclaimed a few mornings later. "Wonderful!" his wife responded. "It will be like a second honeymoon." So off they went for two carefree weeks of sightseeing and relaxing under the Caribbean sun.

Little did my friend know that he was enjoying what experts on aging call "The Honeymoon Period" of retirement. Most discover that those first weeks, with their freedom from responsibility, are pure bliss. But after that "vacation," Carl found he had begun to feel "a bit lonely." So he decided to visit his former office.

Everyone seemed delighted to see him. They said things like, "Why, you haven't changed a bit," or "Where did you get that tan?" or "Hey, guy, I sure envy you retired people—sleeping until ten every day." So Carl decided to visit again the next week. This time, his one-time co-workers had less to say. Once when three or four gathered around him, he saw the supervisor frowning at them and the group soon dispersed. Carl found himself standing alone, and it was then he noticed his former desk. There was a young fellow, "about 25," Carl thought, sitting at "his" desk. "He was punching a computer," said Carl, who had never used one.

Then it dawned on him: His workaday career was over. It was time to let go, to launch a whole new life. "That evening I stared into space and saw many future years staring back at me," Carl confided. "It scared me a little, but I also saw an opportunity for a marvelous future."

My friend was right. He had come to realize that 65+ can be a great time to be alive.

You're Not Old

If you have just turned 65, you have crossed the threshold into what can be an extremely rewarding time. But you must bear in mind two important points. The first is this: start thinking of yourself not as old, but just a little older. Each one of us, of whatever age, is constantly growing older.

You must eliminate the foolish image you may have about being 65+. Don't waste your energy worrying about it. It's just another high-water mark in your life that you can't erase or ignore. As with other milestones in your life, such as when you became a teenager, or hit 21 or 40, being 65+ means you are a little older than you had been before. Take advantage of it instead of bemoaning it, and move on.

I always enjoy the story told about Justice Oliver Wendell Holmes, who, when he was in his 90s, was standing on a street corner in Washington listening to a serious point being made by a colleague when a pretty girl walked by. Justice Holmes turned, watched her pass out of view, sighed, and said, "Oh, to be 70 again."

The French singer and actor Maurice Chevalier attested to the benefits of being 70. He reported that "when you hit 70 you eat better, you sleep sounder, you feel more alive than when you were 30."

Look to the Future

The second point to remember is that, regardless of age, you are an individual in a free country. And, as such, your future is in your hands.

Every retiree at age 65, on average, is staring into a future of 20 active years. What should he or she do with them? As my friend Carl must have wondered at first, "What's so great about my future?"

For nearly everyone, the answer must be *freedom.* Freedom to do those things you've always wanted to do. Freedom to garden, take up woodworking, go back to school for a high school or college degree, travel, grow roses, paint, invent things, study investing, take a course in interior decorating, start an entirely new vocation. You name it—you can do it.

Incidentally, let's not forget that the time in which we live—the 1980s—is a great time to be alive, particularly for those 65+. Think what life was like for the elderly in the first part of this century. Actually, that might be a little difficult to imagine because in 1910, when Halley's Comet flew by, the average life expectancy was

50. The population in America then was 92 million and only 4 million lived to be 65 or older, or just 4.3 percent of the population. Today, seniors total approximately 30 million out of a population of 240 million.

So, you see, you have chosen an exciting period in which to turn 65. For one thing, on average, we live longer today, thanks to the many modern medical advances. There are cures for certain kinds of cancer; drugs and open-heart surgery for heart disease; medicines and treatment for many chronic diseases that beset the aged, such as high blood pressure, arthritis and hardening of the arteries. And there are various implants that make life more comfortable for seniors: lenses for cataract patients and artificial joints for crumbling knees and hips.

Enhanced Living

Though some criticize Social Security, the fact is that this program has kept millions of Americans from poverty in their later years and has enhanced the lives of others living on pensions and modest personal funds.

Today's oldsters are also benefiting from the concern of leaders and societal pressures of the past few years. I am proud to say that when I was Director of the Ohio Commission on Aging, Governor James Rhodes and I instituted the Golden Buckeye Card in our state. With the cooperation of the business community, seniors are able to enjoy discount prices on many services and commodities. So successful was the plan, it has been picked up and adopted all over the country. Similar programs confer lower property taxes on seniors and reductions in their utility bills.

Because seniors have increased in numbers and live

longer, senior centers have been a natural development. Almost any day of the week, seniors can get together there and socialize, pursue or learn a hobby or craft, or just read and relax. Most of all, they are not lonely or isolated, as so often was the case with seniors in former times. If they wish to travel for enjoyment or to visit family or friends, seniors often are given discount rates for airplane and bus tickets.

Seniors are given much more recognition today, as well. Some churches and schools have programs in which senior citizens are honored or invited to give first-hand testimony to the happenings of their generation. And in Ohio, we have created a Senior Citizens' Hall of Fame to honor seniors who have made outstanding contributions since turning 60 or have continued services begun during their careers.

One could continue with this listing of boons seniors today enjoy, but surely the point is made: For those over 65 the '80s are a great time to be alive.

Life Is for Living

After 65, the pressure of earning a living is off, and you can start to live a freer, more elective life. Remember the words of B.C. Forbes, founder and publisher of *Forbes* magazine: "Don't forget until too late that the business of life is not business, but living."

Of course, some persons hearing this might say, in effect, "That might be true, but in my case"—and then comes a tale of woe. There are exceptions, to be sure. Some individuals, for reasons of inadequate income, health impairment or personal inadequacies, will have to work harder at their new life than others. But when you consider the privilege we have been given by these extra years, you realize it is up to you to see that being 65+ is a great time to be alive.

A number of years ago, when I served as Director of the Ohio Department of Mental Hygiene and Correction, I participated in a high school graduation ceremony, incidentally one of the first in the country in a prison setting.

What would you have said to a class of high school graduates who were "serving time" because of crimes against society? I decided to quote the first few lines of Hamlet's soliloquy:

To be, or not to be, that is the question,
Whether 'tis nobler in the mind to suffer
The slings and arrows of outrageous fortune,
Or to take arms against a sea of troubles,
And by opposing end them.

The Superintendent of the Ohio Department of Education used as his theme the following quotation of ten two-letter words. "If it is to be, it is up to me."

We Make the Choice

In both quotations, our emphasis was that, regardless of the handicaps, the problems, the difficulties each of those graduates might feel they had, their future was in their individual hands. And so it is with those of us 65+, whether it will be a great time to be alive is up to us. We make the choice!

This calls for a conscious decision on your part, as it did for the indomitable Arthur Rubinstein, the great pianist. In his memoir entitled *My Young Years*, Rubinstein relates how in his youth he reached the lowest point in his life and attempted suicide. Out of that unhappy experience Rubinstein evolved his philosophy of living: "Love life for better or for worse, *unconditionally.*" As a result, in old age, he took pride in stating, "I still am the happiest person I have ever met" and went on to explain, "Life can deprive us of freedom, of health, of fortune, of friends, of family, of success, but cannot take away from us our thoughts or our imagination, and there is always love, music, art, flowers and books. And the passionate *interest* in everything."[2]

As I have been meeting with older persons over the past 20 years, I have been overwhelmed and humbled by the many ordinary older persons who believe in the philosophy expressed by Mr. Rubinstein.

Meet Carrie

There are few who awaken early each day of their lives and at once take note of a brilliant summer day or rain-laden clouds or heavens dark with a brewing winter storm. This, however, is what Carrie does as part of her daily job—without pay. She has been at this volunteer work as a United States Weather Observer since the first day of April 1946. At 92 she is the oldest weather observer in the United States. Carrie makes meticulous records of the temperature and precipitation in exquisitely penned notations at seven each morning, then mails her observations to the National Service Forecast offices.

As she states, "I have no plans to stop. I'll keep on taking my readings as long as I can, and as long as I can get them to the Post Office."

In reply to a comment about her energy and spritely movements, she states, "I'm all of ninety pounds and about five feet tall, with heels, and I haven't been to a doctor in years and years. I know people just marvel at me because I'm so active, but I think the good Lord has spared me for some reason—I believe this—and I've improved myself every minute of my life."

Another pert and saucy senior citizen at 71 was elected mayor of her village. She readily admits to being a senior citizen and doesn't hesitate to give advice to "others my age."

Her advice? "Stay active. It's important. I think too many people are prone to sit around and say they're too old and can't do anything. But they can! As long as you're able to walk and talk you can do anything. You can do anything you want if you try hard enough. It makes me feel real good to be able to do something for somebody, even if it's just a little thing."

If you would ask both of these people, "Are the 65+ years a great time to be alive?", they would answer with a resounding "Yes." You will find many just like them in this book—men and women age 65+ who are finding happiness and fulfillment in their new plateau of life.

2

65+—A New Generation Profile

"You've reached the magic age . . ."

————————

An artist I know, commenting on the fame that came to him in his early 60s, confided to me, "I'll tell you a secret. Half the fun was getting here." That's true for most of us. The struggle to achieve a goal can be exhilarating; it can be satisfying to look back and see what obstacles you've overcome to get where you are. But notice that my friend also implied that the second part of his life—in his case, lit up by his new-won fame—remained to be enjoyed.

As a member of the New 65+ Generation, this is what you have ahead of you, too: the enjoyment of the years of freedom that you have earned through living. You've reached the magic age that divides your former working life from a whole new period of opportunity for active living.

Perhaps if you are just turning 65, you don't quite see it that way. Out there somewhere, you say to yourself, is the Grim Reaper waiting for me. Of course! But that's always been true, and he waits for all of us. As my painter friend said on another occasion, "None of us is getting out of this alive." What's needed is the strength to face the remaining years with courage and creativity and make the most of them. Do as one older American said on the day he joined the Peace Corps: "I asked the Lord to help me make my last years the best years."

You will have the courage to make the most of your remaining years, I know, for I am aware of the difficulties you have faced in the last 40 or 50 years. Here's how it went for one new 65+er—and it was typical of how it went for many of us.

John's Story

Born in 1920, John was a child of that exciting period of cultural ferment known as the "Roaring '20s," but he remembers little about it. He recalls the '30s better, that time of patched pants and his father working two days a week, sometimes. He was 21 when Pearl Harbor came and he served four years in the Army, saw a great deal of Europe and of human suffering. Thanks to the G.I. Bill, John was able to further his education after discharge, and was a serious student, being older and already married by then. He took a job later than most of today's young do; worked every day of his life; raised a family. Even then, he lived through some pretty stressful times: the Korean War, the Cuban Missile Crisis, Vietnam with its antiwar demonstrations, Civil Rights marches, and all the rest. But he's done pretty well, and he and his wife have a family and grandchildren to show for their years.

John's wife, Helen, shared many of his experiences and did her part in the war effort by working in an armament factory and doing a variety of volunteer services. They both saw the advent of television, stereos, FM radio, computers, jet planes, and two cars and a boat in every garage. She was also the beneficiary of numerous household labor-saving devices: automatic washers and dryers, ironers, no-iron and drip-dry fabrics, cleaning equipment, oven timers, and microwaves. These, together with the Women's Movement, put Helen again into the work force and made the couple a two-income family.

"It's given us a better life, though we pay a lot more taxes and Social Security payments than we ever did," Helen says.

A Longevity Revolution

Perhaps unnoticed by them and by many of us, because of concern and involvement in day-to-day living, Americans aged 65 and older are, and have been, a part of a Longevity Revolution. This term was coined by Dr. Robert N. Butler, first director of the National Institute on Aging and author of the Pulitzer Prize-winning book, *Why Survive? Being Old in America.* As evidence of this revolution, Dr. Butler points out that in just the last 85 years, life expectancy in Western industrialized countries increased more than 25 years. In 1776, Americans lived to an average age of 35. By 1900, it was 47. And when Social Security was enacted in 1935, it was 61. By 1985, life expectancy at birth was 75—or, more accurately, 72 for men, 79 for women.[1]

(Let me make clear that Dr. Butler is talking here about life *expectancy* and not life *span.* Life span is the maximum survival potential of a particular species. "For human beings, there is documented survival of between 110 and 115 years," according to Drs. Edward L. Schneider and Jacob A. Brody of the National Institute on Aging, writing in *The New England Journal of Medicine.* In other words, it is possible to live to those ages, though few do. Life expectancy, on the other hand, is the average observed years of life from birth or from any age. Life expectancy in America keeps moving up, for various reasons.)

As a result, there are a lot more of us: 28,530,000 Americans aged 65+, according to the U.S. Census Bureau's mid-decade update. In fact, we represent just under 12 percent of the 240 million people in this country. Or, to put it another way, one out of every eight Americans is age 65 or older. Thanks to improving health care and other factors, the 65+ population is expected to grow to more than 31 million by 1990. Moreover, "the graying of America" is not just a picturesque journalistic term: the second fastest-growing age group in the United States is the 85+ contingent, rising 21 percent from 2,240,000 in 1980 to 2,711,000 in 1985.

As the one who began Ohio's programs for older persons by establishing the Administration on Aging in 1965, I have witnessed this surge in numbers of the 65+ population. In fact, over the last 20 years, the number of men and women aged 65+ has risen approximately 57 percent. But more than that, each year sees healthier, better educated, more mobile, more articulate older people. They've been more places, they've read more, they've had a better life than their parents, and they are less willing to give up their accustomed life upon retirement. In a strange way, it looks as though today's older people are getting younger.

A Longer, More Healthful Life

Today's seniors can look forward to a life after age 65 longer than ever before. And not only a longer life but a more healthful one, permitting the continuation of an active lifestyle. "A reasonable goal for a life is 100 years," says Dr. William J. Hazzard, director of the Center on Aging at Johns Hopkins Medical Center in Baltimore. When more medical riddles are solved, he added, a life span of 120 years may be possible.

Many other physician scientists have expressed similar thoughts. Moreover, Norman Cousins, whom I've quoted in another chapter and who serves as a lecturer at the School of Medicine, University of California at Los Angeles, and is consulting editor of *Man and Medicine*, published at the College of Physicians and Surgeons, Columbia University, states that everyone "must convince the elderly that the way they look at old age is crucial to their youth and productivity." Further, he states that it is now "a reasonable expectation that humans can live to 120 years, not as vegetables but as productive, joyous human beings. We will do this by persuading the elderly they have a range of reasonable expectations that they can live joyous, helpful, productive lives."

These statements merely confirm what we find in the Bible. In Genesis 6:3 God is speaking to man and says, ". . . My spirit will not contend with man forever, for he is mortal; his days will be one hundred and twenty years."

Great Expectations

There you have it. We're a pretty healthy group, with great expectations for us and those who follow us. Trouble is, many see us as decrepit. Senility is not an inevitable consequence of normal aging, insists Dr. Butler. "It affects only a minority of the elderly." Many who pass the 65 mark think that the nursing home is just around the corner, and they fear the gradual decline it represents.

Dr. Butler gives the lie to that, too. "It is not inevitable that most seniors will have to end up in a nursing home," he declares. "Almost three-fourths of those who survive past 65 will *not* end up in nursing homes." More strikingly, he adds that "half of all nursing home beds could be emptied if science found the solution to Alzheimer's disease," the progressive brain disorder that chiefly afflicts the elderly.

How are those 65+ doing financially? Well, better than we were, but not as well as we might, on the average. In an editorial headed "Don't Give Retirees Cost-of-Living Hike," *USA Today* perhaps said it best. "Conceived in the Depression," the editors wrote, "it (the Social Security System) has transformed the retired from the poorest group in the USA to the least poverty-stricken." Faint praise indeed. The editorial goes on to note that "those in the 65–74 age group make an average of $18,000 a year and have $65,000 in financial assets."

On the same Opinion Page, Senator John Heinz, chairman of the Senate Special Committee on Aging, gave his views on the program that is still the chief retirement plan for an overwhelming number of Americans. "Social Security," Senator Heinz wrote, "has not created a generation of wealthy retirees." Citing census data, he contends that, "even with Social Security, *three-quarters* of all elderly households have *no* discretionary income after meeting basic expenses" (italics his).

Still, from my experience, I can tell you that those 65+ are doing much better than they did some years ago. Seniors annually receive cost-of-living increases in their Social Security checks, government programs reduce their property taxes and utility bills, and they have been able to create their own pension plans through government programs such as the Individual Retirement Account and the Keogh Plan. More seniors than ever before are retiring before age 65, and many continue to work part-time. In thinking about the finances of the elderly, we must remember that figures such as *USA Today* cites are averages.

Gains enjoyed by today's seniors are likely to continue, even expand. Why? Because we represent an awesome political force. Studies have confirmed that seniors vote more often, and are more likely to write their congressmen than any other age group. To put it another way, senior citizens as a group have the highest percentage of voters. Other age brackets have more people, but they don't vote in the same proportions.

So much for this brief profile of the New 65+ Generation. Like a graduation class, it's good to know who we are, where we've been and what we've accomplished. But now it's time to face the future, and that is something each individual does for himself, within the context of family and community. Let us leave this profile chapter with this thought: Each of us is part of a group, 65+—the New Generation; but each of us is also an individual, a unique person, capable of growth, learning, and love. How to make the most of that individual during a very special time of life is what this book is all about.

3

Renewal—Not Retirement

It Can Be a Second Spring

"Or, better yet, the self renewal years."

English is a wonderful language: flexible as a willow wand, euphonious as rain on a pond, utilitarian as a nickel. It has given us the plays of William Shakespeare, the novels of Thomas Wolfe, the speeches of Franklin Roosevelt and Winston Churchill. But like all languages, ours has its occasional weaknesses. We have no good synonym for the French *adieu*, for instance, or the German *auf Wiedersehen*. We say, "The contract *contains* inappropriate language" simply because we have no good substitute for the word; not even *includes* or *presents*.

What makes me think of all this is the word *retirement*. Once it had a meaning accepted by most people, particularly senior citizens (another lapse in our language, by the way). My dictionary gives several definitions for *retirement*, the most pertinent being: "removal or withdrawal from service, office or business"; another is "withdrawal into privacy or seclusion." For many years those were acceptable definitions, because that is what people did at age 65: they withdrew from their office or plant or store and sat down on the back porch to await the inevitable. Today, perhaps, we need a new term to describe what 65+ers do with the remainder of their lives, which can stretch out for 20 or more years, God willing.

A Second Spring

The retirement years, it seems to me, can be like a second spring, which, in fact, does occur in nature each autumn. It is a time when the heavy heat and humidity of summer give way to mellow sunlight and warm days and cooler, earlier evenings. Roses bloom anew, as do the fall flowers and new-planted grasses. So let's compare these years to the second spring of autumn and call them the *renewal years.* Or, better yet, the *self*-renewal years.

Of course, we mustn't be too hard on the language in this regard. What has happened is that our society, with substantial help from today's seniors, has changed the whole concept of retirement and made it a period of growth and opportunity, rather than a time to languish and simply grow old. For many Americans, retirement was once a time to be feared. At age 65, one's income suddenly dropped, with the regular paycheck disappearing and in its place a small pension and a meager Social Security check. Thousands of elderly lived below the poverty line. Health became a major problem for many. Because of one or both of these factors—income and health—older mothers and fathers moved in with their children, oftentimes creating hardships for everyone.

And there was an inevitable loss of status that no longer being among the employed brought with it.

Today, for most persons over 65, much of that has changed. Social Security increases, abetted by rising pensions and savings, have helped bring most seniors to a reasonable level of income. The advent of retirement communities and independent living facilities has helped solve the housing problems of elders and their families. There have been tremendous advances in health care, and Medicare pays for much of the treatment needed by today's seniors. In an article published in 1967 in *Think* magazine, John Gardner, secretary of the then U.S. Department of Health, Education and Welfare, listed "four paramount problems" people of retirement age had to face: income, health, appropriate housing and living arrangements, and interest and purpose in life.

It's a Matter of Attitude

Now, nearly 20 years later, we can reflect that we've done pretty well with the first three problems, though improvements still are possible. And we're doing better on the fourth problem—interest and purpose in life—as the case histories and stories in this book demonstrate. From age 65 on, it's a matter of attitude, of how you think about yourself and your life.

Of course, as I have said before, we are all different; no two of us think exactly alike. Some will want to work till the day they're forced to quit. Some will want to play shuffleboard; others will be content to watch. Some will want to stay at home; others will prefer to be up and going. Some will strive to be a part of their community; others will choose to be left alone. Yet, no matter how different, each of us has basic human needs—for some kind of status, for friendship and socializing, and, most important of all, a purpose in life.

Signs of Age

But, you may say, I'm growing old. I'm over 65. Today that's not considered old. But you will grow old if:

1. You don't have something to get up for in the morning.

2. You don't decide, I have been blessed with a new life. Not in the same way as a baby in mother's arms, but a new life at 65+ with all my hard-won experience and knowledge at my command.

3. You don't find enjoyment in all the things about you.

4. You don't take pleasure in meeting new people and in showing an interest in them—not just your age group but all ages.

The first thing for the new 65+er to do is to take stock of where you are. The fact is, your original working life is over. Either you arrived at the station in life you wanted or you didn't; it's too late to become a vice president, foreman, or a surgeon. Your children, if any, are probably grown and gone off to form their own lives. And there may be other things to accept: physical changes, perhaps disabilities, and an entirely new pattern of life.

Look at Lillian

For many, simple acceptance of these changes may bring pleasure. In her book, *The Shape of a Year*, Jean Hersey quotes a friend named Lillian as saying, "You know, growing old is quite a relief." Lillian was a painter. During her career, she admitted, she wanted to be a great painter. She really tried hard to become one, she told Jean. But in old age she realized she never would be famous and said, "I couldn't care less. These days I paint for pleasure, and it is much more satisfying."[1]

Now, I'm not suggesting that you adopt acceptance as a way of life. It would be easy to sit back and lament, "Oh, well, my life is about over, why fight it? Why strive to have a nice garden, to do physical exercises, to start a new hobby, a whole new career? Why not just go ahead and exist until I pass on?" No, I'm not suggesting that. Notice, in fact, that Lillian did not give up painting; she merely ceased the struggle for greatness, and thereby found greater satisfaction in her painting. Grandma Moses, I suspect, did the same thing: she accepted that her life as a farm wife was consummated, now she could please herself in painting the primitive but charming scenes that made her famous.

So accept your new life, and if you can, turn it into a thing of beauty and a joy forever.

Grow

If there is a formula for this, it can be summed up in one word: *Grow.*

Edward Willis, upon his retirement as principal of East High School in Columbus, Ohio, gave an interview in which he stated the one-line advice he gave his students. "Unless you're learning," he told them, "you're not living."

Coincidentally, within days of that interview, the

same thought was expressed by Leslie Wexner, founder and chairman of The Limited stores, in his commencement address before the Class of 1986 at Ohio State University. Before an audience of some 40,000 people in Ohio Stadium, Wexner advised "to be what we can be . . . to learn, to grow, to prepare for the future, to enrich our lives." Superb advice for graduating seniors and for senior citizens commencing their new lives. Later in the speech, Wexner had more to say on the subject, again appropriate to the senior citizen. "If you stop learning, you stop growing. If you stop growing, then you die." Offering his personal philosophy to the graduates, the business leader concluded with: "Most of all, I believe in dreams, which means I believe in the future."

Some people speak of *growing* old, but author May Sarton seems to question the use of the word in that connection. In *The House by the Sea*, Sarton writes: "*Growing* old . . . what is the opposite of 'growing'? I ask myself. 'Withering' perhaps? It is, I assume, quite easy to wither into old age, and hard to grow into it."[2]

Why Read?

Difficult, perhaps; but not impossible. Many grow old and develop as individuals at the same time. Supreme Court Justice Oliver Wendell Holmes was one of these. The story is told that Franklin Delano Roosevelt, after his inauguration in 1933, paid a courtesy call on the retired jurist, then over 90, and found him in his study reading Plato. President Roosevelt asked him why he was reading the Greek philosopher. Mr. Holmes, it is said, replied, "To improve my mind, Mr. President."

Build on Current Interests

Perhaps the most easily applied blueprint for growth is to build on current interests. One woman who did just that developed a small business around her interest in herb cooking. A retired attorney and librarian, this multitalented woman was also a good cook. After her retirement, Mrs. C. became interested in herbs, and also being a gardener, began to grow various herbs: rosemary, parsley, sage, thyme, and others. Next she looked through her cookbooks for recipes utilizing herbs and tried a few. Eventually she even invented her own herbal dishes. Her family seemed to like them, so she started to give small luncheons and dinner parties for friends, who enjoyed her cookery enormously. These same friends were willing to pay her to prepare herb-garnished luncheons for special occasions. In time, Mrs. C. found she had created quite a reputation for herself, was making some extra spending money, and most importantly, was enjoying herself immensely.

This true story could be repeated many times about other seniors who have built retirement occupations on the foundation of current interests. To wit: The man who discovers a treasure trove of family pictures and letters and becomes interested in writing a genealogy. The couple who find their friends and neighbors have an interest in a variety of subjects, and develop a series of do-it-yourself "college seminars." The couple who have a dual interest in art and travel and, over time, visit many of the art museums around the country. The man with many grandchildren who made it practically an avocation to entertain and teach them, taking them one by one on trips and visits to museums. And then there was the children's librarian who so enjoyed books and children, she started a small children's bookstore in her home after retirement.

A Second Career

For many, the renewal years will open up the opportunity for a second career. This will become more and more common, I predict, since early retirement is a growing phenomenon. Many are now retiring at 62, rather than the traditional 65. In fact, about 20 percent of those between 55 and 59 leave the work force. Thanks to medical advances, these men and women can look forward to a longer, more vigorous old age. Many who retire in their 50s see this as an opportunity to begin a whole new career.

During my years in the field of aging in Ohio, I heard of many such individuals who started exciting, satisfying second careers. Let me give you a few examples:

• Dominick Labino was a vice president for research for a major glassmaking corporation in Toledo, Ohio. In that capacity, he directed numerous scientific studies and experiments. Retired early, he took up a second career as a glassblower. Not only did he have the scientific knowledge needed, he found he had innate artistic ability. He became such a fine artist his glass pieces have been acquired by museums around the country.

• A schoolteacher retired early, but found she missed being with children. Because of the nature of her calling, she had always been rather a dignified person, but down deep she always wanted to be a clown. So she went to a clown school (yes, there really is such a place) and learned all about make-up and how to be a good clown. Now she performs at parties, schools, children's hospitals—wherever there are children to be entertained.

• A mail carrier retired early. But he yearned for those qualities that a job provides: a social environment, friends, a purpose in life. He also missed the out-of-doors. "Those four walls (of my living room) began to seem like a prison to me," the ex-postman told me. So he got a job pumping gas at a neighborhood service station. He confided to me that he's now enjoying life, being out in all kinds of weather and meeting and talking to people.

• Dentists seem to like to try something different from their rather stationary occupation. One dentist of my acquaintance moved to Florida and became a real estate agent. For years another dentist friend had enjoyed his annual vacation trips to Florida to go deep-sea fishing. When he retired he bought a boat in Florida and set up a fishing excursion business. Thus he was able to go fishing every day and be with people, whom he enjoyed.

Notice that most of these people didn't simply continue their former occupations, although their new careers might draw on some of the same skills and personal interests. And I think that's fine. Retirement ought to be a time of taking a new tack, as the winds of change dictate. As you perhaps did early in your working life, you need to sample various ways of spending your days. Try something new even if you're not sure it's for you. Life can be new and exciting and fun, perhaps more so than when you were 20 and just starting out. Only this time you have less to lose, if anything. Try new pathways, meet new people, look for new horizons.

Be Willing to Risk

Does this mean taking risks? Of course! To start in a whole new direction, to launch a second career may call for an investment of time, energy, expertise, perhaps some money. But the rewards can be worth the risks.

In her book *The Touch of the Earth* Jean Hersey has this to say about risk-taking: "Taking risks doesn't always lead to comfort but it invariably leads to aliveness and happenings. The willingness to venture forth . . . opens us to new directions and ways . . . . Taking risks keeps you at the growing edge of living and brings a freshness to your days."[3]

Does all this sound impossible? Does it surpass your comprehension that you could start a whole new life at age 65 or later? Does a second career sound beyond belief? Then let me remind you of the story of Roger Bannister and the four-minute mile. As you may remember (I can say that, since I know you and I remember the 1940s and 1950s), for years the running of a mile in less than four minutes stood as a seemingly insurmountable barrier for athletes the world over. Then, on 6 May 1954, Roger Bannister, an English athlete, became the first to break the record. His time: 3 minutes, 59.4 seconds. Then, the incredible began happening. Runner after runner went on not only to surpass the four minutes, they beat Bannister's record.

What Bannister did, apparently, was to break a psychological barrier among runners that said, "This can't be done." Bannister's spectacular run replied, "This *can* be done."

Who knows, even though you are 65+, you may well be in the springtime of the best part of your life. Go for it!

4

Everyone Is Different—Vive la Difference!

"You will continue to be yourself—an individual."

JOHN: Your mother is getting up in years. I hope she doesn't become one of those cranky old ladies.

JANET: Not a chance. We Joneses have always been individuals with happy, optimistic dispositions.

Janet has the right idea. As we cross the threshold to the 65+ Generation, we don't become homogenized and all take on the same characteristics. On the contrary, if you have had a pleasant disposition when you were younger, the odds are that you will be of happy disposition when you are 65+. Character traits formed during your first 65 years are not going to be readily changed when you become a part of the new generation. You will continue to be yourself—an individual.

Scientific research supports the foregoing claim. It is, in fact, a finding of the Baltimore Longitudinal Study on Aging (BLSA), carried on for nearly 30 years by the National Institute on Aging. Since 1958, this major project has been studying the aging of some 650 volunteers (now grown to a corps of 1,500 men and women) to learn all that is possible about the aging process in humans. According to Richard Greulich, Ph.D., director of the BLSA, research shows that "different body systems vary greatly in rates of change, and BLSA volunteers have wide individual differences as they age." Yet, Dr. Greulich continues, "basic personality features do not change significantly with age and are not influenced greatly by life changes among healthy individuals."

The Best Is Yet to Be

It is to be expected that some of us are afraid of growing old; others accept it as a natural part of life. But regardless of how you may look at it, you're there—you're a part of the new generation, being given a chance for a *whole* life, as stated so well by the English poet Robert Browning in his poem "Rabbi Ben Ezra":

> Grow old along with me!
>   The best is yet to be,
> The last of life, for which the first was made:
>   Our times are in His hand
> Who saith, "A whole I planned,
> Youth shows but half; trust God: see all,
>   nor be afraid!"

Not only are those of us 65+ being given an opportunity for a whole life, as Browning states it so well, but a chance to express that "last of life, for which the first was made" in our own individual way.

One of the stimulations of my own life has come from my involvement in programs directed toward older persons. I've met many 65+ers who enjoy happy, fulfilling, and rewarding lives. Their lives are truly inspiring.

Of course, we hear and read most about the men and women of talent, ability, and fortitude who are lauded for their outstanding achievements. This is as it should be, for we need heroes—we need the inspiration of their success stories. People such as artist Grandma Moses, President Ronald Reagan, surgeon Michael De-Bakey, Sir Winston Churchill, Senator Claude Pepper, comedians Bob Hope and George Burns, actresses Helen Hayes and Lillian Gish, and dozens of others are inspiring role models.

The Quiet Heroes

Many 65+ers will immediately react by suggesting that you can expect outstanding achievements from such a group because they're important, have special talent, greater opportunities, or whatever. But we know that the fabric of the greatness of America is sewn by equally outstanding examples of ordinary men and women who attain success yet are never singled out for it. There are literally hundreds of thousands of 65+ers who are making significant contributions and who are making a difference in their communities.

But because we are individuals, our ways of expressing our individuality will take different forms. Some will give up and constantly complain about the injustices that beset them—that they're unlucky and always have been, that they've done their part and now it's time to take it easy. They feel life owes them enjoyment.

Others are willing to make a contribution, but don't know how. By age 65, each person thinks he knows himself pretty well, thank you. You have certain interests, certain skills, certain talents. Conversely, you are quick to tell others, "I'm just no good at that, never was." But perhaps that isn't true. After all, psychologists tell us that most people use only about one-tenth of their mental abilities. And, for purposes of our working lives, that one-tenth was enough to make a living, rear a family, and generally get along in the world. But now that our "renewal period" (let's not call it "retirement") is here, we ought to try to use some of the other nine-tenths of our talents.

Ray Does It His Way

Many individuals can adapt to other roles in life, and find a sense of achievement in doing so. This was brought home to me a few years ago. Ray, a friend, was put in charge of the company picnic. In years past, the picnic chairman had simply followed conventional wisdom: He put the fellow from the advertising department in charge of doing a flyer about the picnic and getting the signs painted. The business manager was given responsibility for the funds and ordering the refreshments. A vice president was asked to be the emcee. "Well," Ray said, "the heck with that. Let's try another approach."

And try another approach he did. The business manager presently found himself painting signs; the advertising artist had to operate a computer and supervise the refreshment stand; the vice president was obliged to organize the sack race and participate himself. The picnic that year took on an entirely different air. There was a little fumbling and bumbling at times, but everyone seemed to have a wonderful time. No longer was the picnic merely an extension of the committeeperson's daily job, it was a whole new experience.

"We loved it!" one man exclaimed.

Commented another: "We learned a little about what the other fellow has to do to make a living. We gained an appreciation of everyone else's work."

The point here is that each found he had abilities which had nothing to do with his workaday life. He discovered he had talents he didn't know he had. All that was needed was the willingness to set aside conventional logic for a time, to be open to new experiences.

So find out what *you* can do. Don't say, "I can't" until you've tried—and tried hard. Perhaps many years ago a spouse influenced how you performed at something, or a parent or teacher. "Joe always hits his thumb when he makes something," the person would explain. And so you didn't try. Now it's a whole new ball game. Try making something anyway, even if you hit your thumb. Just do it out of anyone else's sight or hearing.

To visit a senior citizens hobby show is a revealing experience. At the last one held in our state, one man had made a car—a red convertible—that ran perfectly. A woman who was blind and deaf produced intricate tatting. And there were numerous exciting productions—paintings, handmade dolls, a tricycle built for two, painted china, embroidery, a dulcimer. The imagination was allowed to run riotously and it was great. Incidentally, the woodcarvings of the late Elijah Pierce, now known internationally, were discovered at an Ohio golden age hobby show.

Tom's Hidden Talent

One story that illustrates my point about hidden talent is that of Tom, a 72-year-old artist who works in silver, copper, and stained glass. When he was a boy, Tom's mother decided his long, slender fingers suited him to be a pianist. But the boy had an aversion to the idea. He took a few lessons, Tom related, but thought piano-playing was "sissified." Instead he became a machinist, a vocation he followed for many years. After he retired, Tom's wife bought him a stained-glass kit for Christmas. "I put it together in two days," he said proudly. Today he produces stained-glass lamp shades, as well as designs and makes silver and copper jewelry. Tom was willing to attempt a new venture, and has fashioned a whole new, satisfying career for himself.

It's Never Too Late

Granted, not everyone will have as much talent as Tom does. The interests of individuals run in many different directions. The point is to try new avenues. One woman I know had always been attracted by the Catholic religion; but because her family and friends were of other religions, they discouraged her from finding out. "I always wanted to know what a Mass was like," she explained to me.

In due course she retired. "Most of my family were gone and some of my friends as well," she said. "I found I could be myself." So one Sunday morning she attended Mass at a nearby Catholic church. She found it a beautiful and inspiring experience.

Similarly, upon his retirement, a college professor I knew decided to begin attending church, something he hadn't done since his youth. There are a number of churches in the little college town and he visited a different one each Sunday. Eventually he decided on the one he liked best.

Real People

Another example of discovering latent interests and abilities: A wealthy woman who had never associated with the poor was asked to participate in her church's meals-for-the-hungry program. She didn't really want to, but finally agreed. She was chagrined to discover these people were not the merely threadbare poor— these were the "street people," the "bag ladies," the really down-and-outers. The woman of means had always thought of such people as "lazy and worthless." But remembering that Jesus was willing to wash the feet of his disciples, this woman served the street people at table. She was astonished, she told me later, to discover that they are "real people, much like the rest of us. They need a kind word, a helping hand." One man expressed a need for a hat. She got one for him. He may have wanted it to keep off the sun and rain, or to be more presentable when looking for work, the woman said, adding, "I didn't ask him."

All the people introduced in this chapter have certain character traits in common: They recognize we are all different, we are all individuals; they realize they may have hidden or unused talents; and they are all willing to change and *grow*. Bless them and all those 65+ who are like them. As the French say (in a slightly different context):

Vive la différence!

5

Myths and Misconceptions

We Have an Image Problem

---

*"Our society . . . has a stereotyped
image of old people."*

——————

Waiting at the traffic light, the young couple in the sports car watched as the old woman made her way across the intersection. On this sunny spring day she wore a sweater, had a shopping bag on one arm, and walked with the aid of a cane. Her progress was slow and the light changed to green before she reached the opposite side. The line of cars was obliged to wait for her for several seconds, which caused some drivers in the rear to honk their horns impatiently. But she did arrive on the other curb and the traffic quickly roared ahead.

The young man driving the sports car had followed with hard, angry eyes the old woman's slow trek across the street. Now as his car spurted ahead, he remarked to his wife: "What right does an old woman like that have to be out by herself? Crippled up like that, too!"

"Yes," his wife replied, "one of these days she'll be killed crossing at that corner."

The young people didn't know it, but they were confirming a stereotyped view of the 65+ generation: that because a person appears old, and is slow-moving or walks with the support of a cane, he or she has no right to be out on the streets alone. For the person's "own good," of course. (If the pedestrian crossing had been a young, pretty girl, the drivers probably would have chuckled and said, "Tsk, tsk, she'd better start sooner next time.")

Now, those of us in the 65+ Generation know that we are all different, that each of us is an individual, and cannot—or should not—be pigeon-holed into a category. But perhaps you have already learned that society wants to categorize us.

Stereotyped by Society

For me, it began when I was in my mid-50s. One day, I became aware that young people, from teenagers through young adults, would open doors for me and allow me to precede them into a restaurant. And a young printing salesman with whom I often did business began to close our telephone conversations with a "Thank you, sir!" It was that "sir" and a bit of extra respect that tipped me off. Not that a little respect is unwelcome—quite the contrary—but it was given because of my increasing age, or so it seemed to me.

For a woman of my acquaintance, her admittance into the society of the aging came upon a visit to a fast-food restaurant. She gave her order, the counter boy punched it into his register, then looked up at her and asked, "Do you have a Golden Buckeye Card?" (This is a discount card issued in Ohio, upon request, to anyone 60 or older and provides for reduced prices at participating stores.) The woman was angry and a little hurt at this request, since she was not yet 60. "Certainly not!" she snapped, inwardly resolving never to come to this restaurant again. It's astonishing what just a touch of gray at the temples will do toward placing you in the category of "the aged."

I have to confess, these experiences prompted me to look for signs of age in others. My dentist, for one. Since I see him only every six months or so, signs of age are rather marked each time I visit his office. Recently I noted that he is becoming rather bent, an occupational hazard, no doubt; and his hair is getting thin. Involuntarily I asked myself, *Am I going to have to get another dentist soon? Is he keeping up on the changes in dentistry, or is he coasting toward retirement?* Then: *Will he outlast me, or will I outlast him?* So you see, it is easy to stereotype anyone beginning to show his or her age.

A Changing Attitude

Once upon a time, in our culture, the elderly used to be respected. Ours was an agrarian society then and the old farmer, no longer head of the house, having given this position over to a son, was often consulted because of his superior knowledge and experience. That, after all, was how knowledge was transferred: by telling or showing how a thing was done. Things like shoeing a horse, making maple syrup, growing field crops, raising or butchering animals, or foretelling the weather. But that day is long past.

Too often, today's young people come out of colleges

and universities with the attitude, "We know what needs to be done. The old ways are inadequate or, even worse, dead wrong."

Some of them say, "Look at the mess the past generation has handed us: wars and their aftermath, the rape of the environment, a huge national debt, racial and social inequalities."

"Why," say these yuppies and Baby Boomers, "today's older people don't even know how to use a computer."

Varied Images

Our society, it seems to me, has a stereotyped image of old people. Like all such stereotypes, this conception varies among people. For some, the "typical" stereotype of the 65+ person might be that of a poorly dressed old man on a park bench; a white-haired grandmother in a rocker, blankly watching television; or a group of seniors in wheelchairs living in a nursing home. Others might see older persons in another way: driving a large, expensive automobile and sporting a Florida tan; a number engaging in a card party or in a golf game at their club; or a happy group enjoying a bus excursion to some scenic or exotic spot.

The fact is, all these images are right—and wrong. There is no "typical" 65+ person who fits a stereotype. There are as many different "images" as there are 65+ persons. Some seniors suffer from inadequate incomes, others get along on modest stipends and a great number are pretty well-off. Some occupy nursing home beds; others live in low-income housing projects or shared-living facilities; still others reside in retirement communities. But the majority are living independently in their own homes or apartments, occupy their time with hobbies, church activities, and volunteer work of all kinds.

Media's Changing Focus

Nevertheless, to some degree, the stereotypes and false impressions of persons 65+ persist, fostered somewhat by the media, although a change is occurring as advertisers begin to recognize the market potential of the older group. Some television shows have perpetuated false images of the 65+ers by playing for laughs. But this, too, is changing as older actors and actresses are depicted in more meaningful roles, and as movies and television shows reflect thoughtful and humorous scenes, not degrading ones purely designed to provide slapstick comedy.

Debunking Other Myths and Misconceptions

Other myths are that "old folks" are set in their ways and can't change their modes of thinking or doing; that older persons are slow-witted and therefore should be handled like children; that seniors, both women and men, are sexless; that they are unproductive and unemployable; that sometimes their physical shortcomings are funny.

Perhaps the first unfortunate stereotype arose in 1884 when German Chancellor Otto von Bismarck, concerned about the growing social discontent, established a pension system to be effective when a worker reached old age. Bismarck set 70 as the original time of retirement, but this was lowered to 65 in 1916, according to Wilbur

Cohen, former secretary of the U.S. Department of Health, Education and Welfare. In either case, the government did not anticipate high expenditures, since only a modest number of workers then lived to these "advanced" ages. In our country, 65 was picked up and used as the benchmark age when the U.S. Social Security System was established in 1935. The point here is that 65 became "old age," even though one may be biologically old before then or not till long after 65.

Another misconception has taken time to correct. This is that most persons 65 or older are in nursing homes or are frail and have severe health problems which restrict their activities. The fact is that no more than 5 percent of all 65+ persons are in nursing homes at any one time. The numbers who have disabling health impairments but do not require nursing home care are difficult to establish. However, it has been estimated that this group is no more than 15 to 20 percent of those 65+. Thus, no more than 25 percent of all persons 65+ are either in nursing homes or have some degree of health impairment. This means 75 percent of us are in relatively good health and more than able to carry on as active members of society.

Another misconception has taken root recently. This is that older persons want everything given to them, that they are always asking for yet another cost of living increase in their Social Security checks, for instance.

Then there is the myth perpetuated by the federal government that a high and ever-increasing percentage of the national budget is devoted to programs for older persons. That is an unfair indictment. True, Social Security is included in the national budget—but it is self-sustaining and not funded from general fund appropriations.

Most older persons are as proud and self-reliant as they were in their younger years. A recent Harris Poll of older Americans concluded with the following consensus:

> Give us less pity and more opportunity. Give us respect not only for having lived so long, but respect born of what we are and still can be. Do not count us out.

I had a similar experience at the 1981 White House Conference on Aging as chairman of one of its 14 workshops. More than 100 resolutions were adopted at this workshop covering a wide variety of subjects, but the last one, accepted unanimously, stated:

> That all delegates and observers stress to senior citizens in their respective states and territories the need for older persons to become more self-reliant and to discover ways to help themselves, thus minimizing their dependence upon Federal, State, and Local assistance programs and services.

Each of us must take the time and trouble to point out to the general public the myths and misconceptions about today's older persons. We must also "accentuate the positive" and show by our actions that we are not to be labeled and placed in categories of obsolescence merely because we are or have passed the age of 65.

Things You Can Do

Here are samples of some of the things we 65+ers can do to help erase the image of the "typical senior citizen":

• If your driving isn't what it used to be, talk to your doctor about it. Possibly you need cataract surgery to correct an eyesight problem. Perhaps you're being over-medicated, making your reactions slow. If the problem isn't physical, consider one of the brush-up courses for older persons, such as the one given by the American Association of Retired Persons and certain insurance companies. You may be able to improve your driving skills and cut your insurance rate at the same time.

• Give 110 percent effort in any volunteer or paid work you may do. Too often, older persons believe that employers will "make allowances for me because I'm old." To the contrary, show them that you're as good or better at the job than any young person.

• Be courteous. Don't take the attitude that because you're old you can say or do whatever you feel like. Curiously, many elderly seem to lose their inhibitions in this regard, boldly "taking the prerogatives of age," as they term it. Remember, courtesy is always in style.

• Don't give in to age. A woman of 80 told me she sometimes wakes in the morning with arthritic pains in her joints and asks herself, "Oh, do I really have to get up today?" But she lies there and thinks how much she enjoys her part-time job as a saleslady. Eventually she scolds, "You won't ache any worse moving around the dress shop than you do right now." And so she rises and goes to work.

• Accept the new medical advances that can benefit your health and most of all your functioning. One man I know, after being deaf for 40 years, had himself fitted with a tiny unobtrusive hearing aid. His family says the transformation has been startling. He knows what's going on around him, can listen to television without blaring the sound (and upsetting the rest of the family), and talks about the news of the day. Much the same thing happens to those who undergo cataract surgery, or have new joints surgically implanted.

- Do as much as you can for yourself. Many oldsters are all too willing to have others do for them, self-righteously saying, "I have it coming to me after all these years." Think how that ruins your image as an independent individual!

- Keep up on current events. It's really not too difficult to stay tuned in to the world. Listen to the radio, read a newspaper, watch TV news, talk to friends and neighbors.

- Don't dress old. Many seniors take the attitude that old people should dress in dark, nondescript clothes. They forget that if you feel old, you'll dress old; and if you feel young, you'll dress young. Of course, don't overdo it; nothing types you as old more quickly than dressing as though you are 16. Incidentally, watch your grooming. A slovenly appearance, too, can type you as old.

- Don't dwell on the past. Sentences that begin "when I was young" tend to turn off the young and type-cast you as old. And don't be too critical of the young: each to his own generation. Besides, it's bad for your image.

Yes, we 65+ers have an image problem, all right. But the situation is improving, and each of us can take steps every day to help prevent the public from categorizing us as "the old." Have you done your part today?

6

Good Health Is Found in Motion

Physical, Mental, Spiritual

"Running water does not stagnate."

Since, as many believe, humor is good for what ails you, let's begin this chapter with a witticism from comedian George Burns, who is now over 90. I once heard George say in a television monologue, "If I'd known I was going to live this long, I would have taken better care of myself." That's funny—and it's also how many of us seniors feel as we grow ever older and experience the health problems of aging.

However, I submit there is much older persons can do to improve their health even as they age. Surviving to one's genetic potential can be accomplished through the body, the mind, and the spirit.

I once had the opportunity of listening to geriatricians from different countries discuss the status of aging programs and research in their respective homelands. A very interesting comment came from the physician from the Peoples Republic of China, a country which historically has paid attention to its aged people. One of his teachings was "Good health is found in motion," which he said was found in records dating back to 700 B.C. To illustrate his point he cited that, "Running water does not stagnate." This reminded me of a belief, expressed by Dr. Norman Vincent Peale, well-known man of God and author of *The Power of Positive Thinking*, a book whose philosophy I have tried to follow in my own life. Said Dr. Peale: "God intended each one of us to grow; growth is built into life. The grass grows and when it stops growing it withers. While it is growing it is healthy, full of energy. Human beings are like that, too. While they grow they have life and energy. But when they stop growing health begins to wither."[1]

Growth suggests motion and so the battle cry of the New Generation-65+ should be "Good Health Is Found in Motion" as it applies to body, mind, and spirit.

Physical Exercise

Motion applied to the body means physical exercise and most of us recoil at the very thought. Yet more doctors seem to agree on the benefits of following some form of physical exercise, whatever your age. However, for older persons, the form and vigor of exercise should be adjusted to the individual's age and physical condition. Thus, before you embark on any kind of strenuous exercise program, talk it over with your personal physician.

Your doctor will probably discourage you from jogging or running. Dr. Irving Wright, a cardiologist and a past president of the American Heart Association and now the president of the American Federation for Aging Research, warns against taking up jogging for the first time after the age of 40. "Frankly," comments Dr. Wright, "my experience says if you haven't done it before, starting at 40 is inviting disaster." Although a strong proponent of remaining physically active all one's life, Dr. Wright thinks walking and swimming are the best exercise.

The Way to Walk

I am an advocate of walking and, in fact, it is really the only physical exercise program I follow. By walking I mean rapid walking in the manner of former President Harry Truman, who popularized the activity in the 1950s. There's something about being outdoors, breathing the outside air, having the breeze, whether warm or cold, touch your face, and feeling the sunshine, that makes you glad to be alive. During your walk, stop periodically and take eight or ten deep breaths. Really breathe deeply, then exhale slowly.

Rest and Reflect

Personally, I also like to stop occasionally to rest and reflect. Thus you are exercising the body and the mind at one and the same time. To be of most benefit, take these walks two or three times weekly, on a regular basis. Incidentally, inclement weather need not be a deterrent to your walk. You can drive to one of our modern enclosed shopping malls and walk there. Some walkers go to the trouble of obtaining a pedometer to measure the distance walked. This is interesting and can be enlightening.

In Ohio a number of years ago, to emphasize the importance of walking as something every 65+er could do, we set aside one day each year for a statewide walk. At a particular time on that date, older persons in every hamlet, village, and city get together and walk a prescribed route, with attendant publicity.

Other Forms of Exercise

Of course, walking or hiking is just one form of exercise for the older person. Others that come to mind are swimming (second only to walking in winning approval of doctors), mowing your lawn (use good judgment: Not in hot sun, not too much at once), gardening (same cautions), dancing (either in a class or social gathering), woodworking or similar hobby that calls for moderate physical effort, biking, golf, badminton, volleyball, skating, work of any kind that keeps you active, such as washing your car, sewing, embroidery, carrying groceries, doing volunteer work.

Let me re-emphasize that the exercise must be proportionate to the health and physical capacity of the individual. For some, the actual mowing of a lawn may be too strenuous. Lawn trimming, on the other hand, may not be, with the action of the hand trimmer being good physical therapy for arthritic finger joints. Again, check with your doctor.

Within reason, the older person should vary his or her exercise program in order to use as many as possible of the vital organs and muscles. Why? Dr. Hans Selye, the internationally renowned scientist, explains the reason in his book *The Stress of Life.* "Aging is not determined by the time elapsed since birth," Dr. Selye writes, "but by the total amount of wear and tear to which the body has been exposed." People seldom die of old age, he continues, because that would imply that all of the body parts have worn out at the same time. Rather, we die because one vital part has worn out and can no longer perform its function in the biological "machine" we call the human body. Thus, Dr. Selye goes on to say, "The human body—like the tires on a car, or the rug on the floor— wears longest when it wears evenly. We can do ourselves a great deal of good in this respect by just yielding to our natural cravings for variety in everyday life. We must not forget that the more we vary our actions the less any one part suffers from attrition."[2]

Keep Your Mind Active

What about "motion" as it applies to the mind?

A New England psychologist once told me: "You can stay young longer by keeping your mind active. It makes no difference whether you're 30 or nearing 70, anyone who's interested in remaining young should realize the most important factor of all is the mind."

Eric Hoffer, the self-educated longshoreman who became quite a philosopher and wrote a number of thought-provoking books, believed in keeping the mind active in the after-work years. "Retirement should be spent in good books, conversation with friends and leisurely study," he wrote.

In her most excellent book, *The Shape of a Year*, Jean Hersey relates how she and her husband Bob combined all three of Hoffer's activities during long winter evenings in New England. First, Bob would build a large fire in their grate, then she would begin hooking her current rug while he read aloud. In the year in question, they studied England, reading, for example, Anya Seton's *Katherine*, a historical novel that is "as thick as a dictionary." Such an idea could well be emulated by today's senior citizens. Two or more seniors could take turns reading whatever they choose. This could develop into an afternoon or evening reading and discussion club.

Another of Hersey's ideas was to study French one winter, preparatory to taking a summer trip to Europe. Again, seniors could do the same thing, using language conversation books and tapes or records. Or, one or more seniors could simply prepare for a trip to San Francisco or Florida by reading the appropriate travel books, histories, or other source books. This can greatly add to the enjoyment of the trip when taken.

Use Your Library

If you are a new retiree, you have probably discovered that older people make up a major group of library-users. They have discovered their local libraries are treasure troves of reading, videotapes, audio records and tapes, newspapers and magazines, even computers. And don't forget the large-print books, which are such a boon to those with failing sight—and "talking books," or books on tape, of which there is an increasing number. Many libraries have discussion or current events groups, and usually a place where the members can meet. If you make full use of your library card, you will enjoy an active mind, I can assure you.

Now, of course, not everyone is a reader. But how you keep your mind active is an individual choice. Other ways might be the development of a hobby, active participation in volunteer programs, or part-time work. The choice is yours. Enjoy!

Some readers are going to resist this advice, saying, "I can't do any 'mind motion' because my memory is failing." Or, "My mind gets tired quickly." Or, "I'm not as young as I used to be." Naturally, because of an organic problem, this can be true with some individuals. But with most of us, it's a matter of laziness—we simply don't want to exert the effort.

Try a Little Harder

According to the Baltimore Longitudinal Study on Aging, carried on under the aegis of the National Institute of Aging, "some cognitive functions (memory, intellectual performance, learning, reasoning) do decline as we grow older." However, the 25-year study showed it was memory loss that was most apparent in older persons. On the other hand, in vocabulary improvement older groups did better than younger ones. But, the study stated, "in each of these functions motivation and extra effort were important factors." In other words, if you're an older person, you have to try a little harder to learn, reason, and remember things. You have to want to and put forth some extra time and effort. But it can be done.

The Brain Is a Muscle—Exercise It!

Read what Hugh Downs, well-known television personality and currently host of the highly regarded television show 20/20, recently had to say in *Private Clubs* magazine: "The brain is a muscle. You've got to keep exercising it. There is often some atrophy there beyond disease—call it flabby brain—that comes from feeling you don't have much to contribute and enjoy."

Last but certainly not least, we also need to keep our souls in motion. For our soul, or the spirit, is of equal importance to the body and mind. Spiritual "motion" must be maintained, as well as the motion of body and mind. Plato said we should never attempt to look after the body without looking after the soul.

The Importance of Love

At various times in our lives all of us have been sustained by our faith. Most of us 65+ers find comfort in our relationship to God, particularly as we begin to realize the days ahead are dwindling. Those with an established "church home" have an opportunity to participate in the ministry of his or her church. Certainly that which we have learned as a part of our religious faith can be applied by us in a more direct way: through love.

For me, one of the most meaningful lines in all the inspirational literature I have read is one written by Dr. Ralph Sockman, widely known as a Methodist minister and author. It reads: "Love is a force from within seeking expression and not a vacuum seeking to be filled."

Let me explain how this applies. It has been my observation that not everyone can say, "I love you" to a mate, a parent, child, brother, sister, or friend. A woman of my acquaintance is like that. The words do not come easily, if at all, to her lips. But she expresses her caring through the things she does for those she loves. She may buy you a present when she is shopping at the supermarket (a pint of strawberries "just for you"), put up curtains in your new office, bring you a book from the library, call to make sure a visitor got home all right, drive blocks out of her way so that a friend can experience the spectacle of a street of flowering trees in the spring. All these kindnesses take extra work or effort on her part. Most often, the beneficences are unexpected, making them all the more welcome. They are all expressions of her love. They touch the spirit.

During my years of public service in Ohio in mental health, I met with many psychiatrists, both in the public and private sectors, and learned from them these truths, so simple and yet so meaningful.

- Every person needs to be loved.
- Every person needs to love someone.

The Need to Be Needed

This recalls to mind a disturbing quotation which I read in Ronald Blythe's insightful book, *The View in Winter*. Blythe quotes the Swiss geriatric apologist Paul Tournier as declaring: "I have come to the conclusion that there is one essential, profound, underlying problem, and it is that the old are not loved. They do not feel themselves to be loved, and too many people treat them with indifference and seek no contact with them." [3] Reading that quotation recalled to me Robert Frost's poem "The Death of the Hired Man." As you may recall, Silas, the aged, dying farm hand, had come back to the farmer and his wife to ditch their meadow. As many old people discover, no one relies on them any more. Even in his last hours, Silas needed to be needed.

Spiritual Exercise

Each of us in the New 65+ Generation can do something about expressing spiritual motion. We can manifest our love toward our fellow man by way of a smile, a pleasant greeting, a sincere compliment. We can keep social contact with family and friends, thereby encouraging theirs with us. Interestingly, a recent study by the National Center for Health Statistics bears out that such social support can help elders live longer. There is evidence, the authors of the study wrote, that "people who have a lot of friends and relatives and who see a lot of them are likely to live longer than those who seldom visit with friends or relatives."

A woman of my acquaintance, who is over 90, once confided to me that each night she prays that she will die in her sleep. Yet this same woman dresses beautifully, loves to read, has just redecorated her apartment, and often goes out to lunch with friends. She really doesn't want to die, in my opinion; she's really pleading, "Care about me. I'm old and lonely; don't abandon me."

As the poet Kahlil Gibran tells us, by doing good deeds for our friends, neighbors, relatives, and others, we express our love. Not only are such actions beneficial to the one who receives them, they also warm the heart and lift the spirit of the person who does the giving.

However, another expression of spiritual motion which should be practiced is the art of silence. You've heard it said, "Speech is silver; silence, golden."

Silence is an important part of spiritual development. Shakespeare wrote in a play, "Silence is the perfectest herald of joy." As persons 65+, we should set aside a time for communion with our God. Of course, we do that when attending a church service or any religious ceremony. But in addition to those occasions, set aside a few minutes a day when you can be alone with God. It can be anywhere—somewhere in the house or outside—but by yourself.

This may not be easy at first, for being alone is difficult for some people. But in time you'll look forward to those moments. Don't be hasty about a judgment in spending time in this manner. In the beginning you'll be impatient, "I've got this to do, etc.," but as you just sit in quiet contemplation a serenity will embrace you, and then the thoughts will flow. Reading your Bible or a good devotional can enhance that meditation period.

Thus, the secret to a longer and more fulfilling life after age 65 is to keep yourself active physically, mentally, and spiritually. Motion—Motion—Motion. Each of them equally important: Body—Mind—Spirit.

7

Be Alive to Stay Alive

---

*"Without a happy, fulfilling life,
longevity is meaningless."*

The headline read: "Happiness of the Elderly New Priority." I had been rummaging through my file of clippings of magazine and newspaper articles about aging, and had run across this Opposite-Editorial Page dated 4 July 1979. An overline on the half-page article added: "View from OSU: Family, Health, Finances Researched." Now, I have no wish to quarrel with the authors of this article, who are fully qualified academics, but it seems to me a vital factor has been left out of their equation: The senior citizen himself/herself. Indeed, I took strong exception to the last paragraph of the article. After predicting the rise in the 65+ population to 55 million by the year 2030, they concluded with this warning:

> Unless our society begins to plan and adapt for this major demographic change soon, these questions will

not be simply academic; they will be vital to the health and well-being of a substantial portion of Americans— the aged and their families.

What disturbs me here is that the problem of the aged is tossed blithely into the laps of "society." What's wrong with seniors taking some responsibility for their own well-being? By so doing, I submit, they will add years to their lives and life to their years.

What that maxim boils down to is good health habits and a better quality of life. As mentioned in the preceding chapter, the best advice I can give you on health is: Be guided by the advice of your physician. He or she knows you best and can give you advice tailored to *you*. No doubt your doctor will tell you to eat right, exercise moderately, don't smoke, keep your weight down, and always get a good night's sleep. If you decide to take up tennis or jogging, I urge you to talk it over with your doctor first. He can help you decide based on your physical capacities. If you've been light on exercise all your life, he may counsel table tennis or an exercise bicycle instead. Perhaps the best rule of good health—whether or not it produces longer life—is moderation in all things.

Quality of Life

So much for health, a very individual matter in any case. Let's move on to quality of life, equally king-sized but just as important to this new plateau of life. Without a happy, fulfilling life, longevity is meaningless.

Thomas Chalmers, the nineteenth century Scottish cleric, once gave this formula for happiness. There are three essentials, he said: "Something to do, something to love, and something to hope for."

If there is one single factor that can make or break quality of life, it is one's spouse. But things can change in retirement. For today's 65+ Generation, the pre-retirement division of labor was quite clear: The men went to work each day; the women, for the most part, stayed home, kept house, and reared the children. But then comes retirement: The men are home every day, expecting life to be one long vacation. The women, meanwhile, find life has changed for them, too, though not necessarily for the better. With the husband home all the time, the wife's days contain more work than ever, and at the same time, she feels more restricted—no more quick trips to the store in the family car (husband has driven it to the golf course), fewer lunches with friends (hubby expects his lunch on the table at 12 sharp), and appointments must be dovetailed with husband's plans ("Can you drop me at the hairdresser's tomorrow, dear?").

Love and Marriage

Clearly, there must be more give and take, more cooperation, a greater effort than ever before to be loving and considerate. Chances are, if you have been good friends and close companions before retirement, all will go well after retirement. But if you've been living in a state of armed truce for years, merely keeping out of each other's way, you're headed for trouble. You may be about to become one of those elderly divorcees you hear about. Still, all may not be lost; it is possible to develop the qualities of love and friendship that make married life enjoyable and productive.

Perhaps just being together for the first time in years may prove the start of a "second wind" for your marriage.

I once knew a man who in mid-life went on a three-week vacation with his wife, without the children. They took a scenic train trip out through the American West. When he came back to work, he reported: "I really got to know my wife. She turned out to be a pretty nice person." Perhaps that's what some of today's retirees will discover about their spouses.

As a matter of fact, today's 65+ couples deserve compliments on their record in the love and marriage department. Every Sunday in our local newspaper there appears a section of golden wedding anniversary announcements with a photo and biographical sketch of each couple. There are usually several of these, but on the Sunday before this chapter was written, there was an entire page of pictures and bios—and it wasn't even a special holiday. Imagine! Fifty years together. Undoubtedly, today's young people could learn something from these couples. Statistically, one of every two young '80s couples end up divorced. It's getting to be chic to be divorced, and even more chic to have two or three children who gravitate between the parents, according to the dictates of a court. No wonder there is so much alcoholism and drugs among our young.

Anyhow, congratulations to the New 65+ Generation! Beyond doubt, you have something to teach today's young about love and marriage—and about quality of life.

Alas, though, nothing lasts forever. If the statistics prove out, the wife will outlast her husband by several years. This means she will have to cope with the problem of being alone for a certain period of time. It will call on all her resources and inventiveness to do so. This is where family can mean so much to the older persons' quality of life.

One morning my wife and I stopped to admire the spectacular display of summer flowers around one of the apartments in a local senior citizen complex. The resident, pleased at our interest, stopped watering the beds long enough to tell us about them. "Each year, on Mother's Day, my daughter brings over several flats of mixed flowers, and together we plant them." She extended both arms to her flower beds. "This is my Mother's Day gift," she said proudly. Neatly dressed in slacks and blouse, she was perhaps 70, not old as seniors go these days. For me, this episode reflected a wonderful quality of optimism, coupled with the enjoyment of living and the love of a mother and a daughter.

Dealing with Loneliness

Of course, sons and daughters and even grandchildren have their own lives to lead—and that's when loneliness can set in. Those of us in the field of aging have seen and read much about the problem of loneliness and know how painful it can be for older people. But you know, there is an antidote for the poison of loneliness: it's called friends and neighbors. All of us know people who we say have a "talent for friendship," and that is what you must develop if you are lonely. That's right, you must make the effort to keep up good relations with family members, neighbors, and others. Above all, you have to take steps to become involved in life.

One way to meet people is to join a church, or attend the one to which you already belong; start going to your senior center; or volunteer at the local hospital, nursing home, or community center. When you find someone who might become a friend, don't be shy about inviting that person to lunch, to a show, or a concert. If you prefer, ask your new friend over for coffee and dessert, to play games or watch television. In your relationships, be flexible. Don't expect to have your own way always. Friendship, like marriage, calls for some give and take. Maybe you like to lunch early, say at 11:30, while your friend prefers lunch at one o'clock. Well, give a little! Compromise on 12:15, if you can; if you can't, then dine at one o'clock. It won't kill you! Just eat dinner a little later, that's all.

Friendship may ruffle the smooth pattern of your life. But is that so bad? It may be exactly what you need. Perhaps the friend loves exercise and you don't like it very much. Again, a compromise may be in order; in this case, a long walk may be the answer. In fact, a walk may do you good. And isn't that bit of inconvenience better than loneliness? Perhaps a woman thinks her friend wears her skirts a bit too short. So what? Perhaps the friend thinks the other woman wears hers a trifle too long. The essence of friendship is that we like our friends in spite of their faults, and are willing to overlook weaknesses or shortcomings, while not necessarily condoning them.

Another thought on being a friend: Pay your way. Don't be one of those people who expects to be picked up and taken to church, shopping, or a show. But you don't have a car, you argue, and your friend does. Well, then, offer to pay for the gasoline. Or bring your friend something you saw in a gift shop window. Don't be a taker, the poor soul who always has to be cared for by others. At the very least be a sharer. Better yet, be a giver.

Perhaps Sam Levenson said it best in his book *In One Era and Out the Other.* Ironically, the quote is from a letter to a newborn grandchild: "As you grow older you will discover that you have two hands. One for helping yourself, the other for helping others."[1]

It's said that you can't teach an old dog new tricks, that a leopard doesn't change its spots. You've heard these clichés, and if you read the previous chapters in this book, you know that I believe older persons can and should change. If you're not learning, you're not growing; and if you're not growing, you're not living. I also believe that growth is enhanced by a positive outlook, laced with a good sense of humor.

Dealing with Illness

There is one school of thought that believes a positive attitude will not only help you keep well, it can cure serious illness. Norman Cousins, who for many years was editor of the influential *Saturday Review,* told in his book *Anatomy of an Illness* how his humor helped him survive an otherwise fatal sickness.[2] Lately, though, I read that the benefits of a positive attitude are still under study by medical researchers. One study says yes, another says no. Yet another study reported in *Modern Maturity* was headlined "Grumps Take Note: You May Live Longer." The study findings were that if you are a grouch you'll outlive the cheerful, good-natured person. Well, for my money, it's okay to be a bit feisty, a person who stands up for his rights—but a grump, never. To go around with a mad-on all the time, presenting a bitter, angry countenance to the world—that's fighting a war, with yourself and with others every day of your life. If that's the answer to longevity, then better to trade a few months of life for a lot of years of happiness.

Nobody ever said getting old is easy. Physical

disabilities can take a lot of fun out of life. But I like the philosophy that turned up in a letter from an elderly friend who had had two heart bypass operations and her left leg amputated. In her letter my friend apologized for her handwriting, remarking that her right thumb and two fingers were numb from the bypass surgery. Nevertheless, she wrote, "It isn't so much what we lose as what we have left that counts."

Looking at the Funny Side

One way to maintain a positive outlook is to try to see the funny side of life when you can. Now, many of us old-timers have a good sense of humor—until it comes to our age and retired station in life. Lately, though, I've been making a collection of cartoons and jokes about aging; and I find that few are out-and-out putdowns. In fact, many of the cartoonists must be older themselves, or have a relative or friend who is. Case in point: Dennis the Menace says to his little friend: "My Dad tells it like it is. But Mr. Wilson always tells it like it *was!*" Another I like is the panel called "The Small Society." In this one, the wife, commenting on her sad-faced, slouched-down-in-his-chair husband remarks, "Hoo-Boy! Talk about nostalgia. You know what he misses? He misses his unhappy childhood." "The Family Circus" is especially good at occasionally including a touching little scene depicting the older generation. In this one, a tiny child is reaching up to show his grandfather a toy robot. The little girl of the family says to her brother: "Old people get bent over so they can look at their grandchildren."

Well, you get the idea. (I've been having a fine time chuckling over these cartoons in my file folder . . .

almost as much fun as I had collecting them.) The point is, we older folks should develop a sense of perspective about our age, enough so that we can take a little ribbing about ourselves. To help you remember, here is a little saying that you can copy and fasten to your refrigerator door:

> Optimism and a Sense of Humor
> Are Good for What Ails You

My next and final topic may seem like an about-face, as it has to do with making bequests in your will. Admittedly, that subject isn't funny. But please go along with me for a moment on this one.

Where There's a Will, There's a Way

If you're like most of us, you've made out a will and left most, if not all, of your life savings to your spouse or children or some close relative. And I'll wager you've willed nothing whatever to some of the organizations and institutions that meant the most to you in life: your church, senior center, or service club. Why do we do that? Just thoughtless, I guess. Or do we take such organizations for granted, feeling they'll get along somehow?

What set me to thinking of this was a little story in the paper about a man named Paul "Pee Wee" Sayanek, who lived in a run-down house in Byesville, Ohio. This 76-year-old bachelor, described by the news reporter as "shaggy and unkempt," set up a $30,000 scholarship fund for needy Guernsey County students. "Money don't mean a thing to me now," he was quoted as saying. The following spring, the first $500 scholarship in his name was to be awarded to a student whose family cannot afford to send him or her to college.

Reading of this admirable gesture made me think of a nurse I once knew. A few months after her retirement she died suddenly, leaving no will. Since she had never married, and had no brothers or sisters, her estate was divided among a number of cousins in another state, people whom she had not seen in years. How much better if she could have done as "Pee Wee" did, perhaps leaving all or part of her life savings of several thousand dollars to a nursing scholarship, a mental health association, her church, or whatever she chose.

I believe the warm feeling such an act—taken toward the end of one's life for the benefit of many, many people who come after—would add life to anyone's years.

8

Use Your Experience and Knowledge for Creative Living

"What, may I ask, are you doing with the experience and knowledge you possess?"

—Age 65 is commonly thought of as the "normal" retirement age. However, almost two-thirds of older workers retire before age 65.

—Three-quarters of the labor force would prefer to continue some kind of part-time work after retirement.

These two statements, drawn from a report entitled *Aging America,* prepared by the U.S. Senate Special Committee on Aging, seem contradictory. Yet they are not. Most of us want to retire as soon as possible; retirement means freedom: to get up when we wish, to do what we want to do, not to have others tell us what to do. Nevertheless, once retired, many 65+ers make an important discovery: It was our work that gave us dignity and an identity. You were not just Bill Smith; you were Bill Smith, businessman, postal worker, or whatever. Many of us want to continue some kind of part-time work, usually in our former occupation, so as to retain our status in life.

You and I have spent a minimum of 65 years to acquire our experience and knowledge. Naturally, our knowledge and experience vary, for each of us is different; each of us had different opportunities, different motivations, different reasons, different circumstances that resulted in whatever we achieved in those first 65 years. However, regardless of our individual achievements as measured by the standards of society, the experience and knowledge we gained belong to us alone. No one can take them away.

"Keep on Working"

Actor and entertainer Mickey Rooney, when addressing the Ohio Governor's Conference on Aging, said in part: "Experience is beautiful. There is nothing to be ashamed of to become *more* experienced. Don't run away from experience—and stop living in the past. It's gone!"

He went on to say, "I'm not quite 65 yet, but I'll be there soon, and I can tell you this: I've been in the motion-picture business for 56 years, and I'm going to keep on working for as long as the public wants me!"

How different is Mickey's approach to retirement compared to a man whom I knew some years ago. Albert was a purchasing agent for a large drug company and an excellent amateur photographer. One evening just before his retirement at age 60, Albert said to me, "I've learned all I'm going to about my hobby. Now I'm going to enjoy it and just use what I know." And what he knew was considerable. Albert had a great deal of equipment, his own darkroom, and was skilled at photographing art objects.

One day, sometime after his retirement, I ran into Albert. He told me he had closed up his darkroom and was selling his equipment. "I guess I've run my course with that hobby," he said, a hint of regret in his voice. I got the impression that photography had ceased to be fun any more for Albert.

Albert had stopped growing and learning in his hobby. And that had been the fun. If you're turning out the same pictures you always did, picking the same subjects, and using the same techniques, you begin to bore yourself. The only answer is to continue to grow and learn all your life.

Don't Let It Rust!

I believe that the skills, the experience, the knowledge that 65+ers have should continue to be used. It should not be permitted to rust away. Alfred Lord Tennyson, the British poet, said it best in his poem, "Ulysses":

> How dull it is to pause,
> To make an end,
> To rust unburnished,
> Not to shine in use,
> As though to breathe were life.

What, may I ask, are you doing with the experience and knowledge you possess? Now, some reading that question will respond, "What I'm doing—or not doing—is no one's business but mine." But is that true? As

Tennyson wrote in his poem, and this particularly applies to 65+ers, "as though to breathe were life." Is that our sole purpose—just to breathe and forget all else?

Think! Think how fortunate you are, no matter what your condition or circumstances. How many of your friends are around to have the opportunity you do of utilizing your experience and knowledge? Think of it! You can use the experience and knowledge gained over a lifetime for the betterment of mankind. To put it another way, I believe the "plus years" after age 65 should be dedicated to God. Not so long ago, I saw a sign in—of all places—a gasoline station that said it so well:

> Your life is God's gift to you,
> What you do with it
> Is your gift to God.

Many individuals live by such a credo. Whether you do or not is a matter of individual conscience. We of the New 65+ Generation are being given an opportunity of dedicating our experience and knowledge to God in appreciation for the blessings with which our lives have been enriched. Painter-philosopher Eric Sloan illuminates in the following passage from his fine little book *The Spirits of '76* why we should not permit our experiences and knowledge to go unused: "A great man is one who believes his life belongs to civilization—that whatever God has bestowed upon him, he . . . automatically gives to mankind."

"Life Is a Relay"

Jesse Owens, who electrified America by winning four gold medals at the 1936 Olympic Games in

Germany, put it a little differently, yet as meaningfully. In addressing a group of senior citizens he said, "We, who have reached the golden age, can give of ourselves to those who are going to lead in the years to come. You have carried the baton of this life as if life is a relay, and you've run your particular part of the relay—and you're going to pass the baton to another generation. You've run it well. Teach the future well."

During our working lives, we put off doing many things, or set them aside, however laudable they might be, because they "don't pay." We had to think of that weekly or monthly paycheck; it represented health and well-being and security for ourselves and our families, so it came ahead of anything else. But in retirement, if we've played our financial cards right, we're free of the tyranny of the paycheck. We can try new things, whether developments of our previous experience, or entirely new, creative approaches to living—things we couldn't afford to do in the past.

Three Case Histories

At this point, let me share with you three case histories of retirees who have chosen to use their knowledge and experience in constructive ways:

Case 1:   This case is really a group of retired school administrators. It is known as SAGES, which stands for Senior Administrators Giving Educational Support. This volunteer corps is a kind of big brother organization founded to provide information and consultation to fledgling as well as experienced school principals. Members of SAGES observe and counsel principals, sometimes serving as sounding boards, other times sharing their experiences in dealing with unruly children, play-ground emergencies, and angry parents. They're also compiling a list of retired principals whom the new prin-cipals can call for advice as needed. As is true with so much volunteer work, the principals get as much satis-faction from their work as they give help. Said one of them: "It has been a pleasure to me to know that I'm helping kids again. And the other retirees are just tick-led to death to help."

Case 2: Grace, a painter, resides in a picturesque Old World community adjacent to the inner city of a large metropolitan area. For years she and her husband and three children lived in a large brick home there. The third-floor garret served as her art studio. But when she reached 75, the large house was becoming too much for her. Fortunately, a home-sharing program that matches older homeowners and young boarders sent her Tracy, a 20-year-old artist and college student. The housing fee that Tracy pays helps cover the high utility bills, and the young woman provides a helping hand around the house for Grace, who has arthritis. Grace, for her part, shares with Tracy her decades of experience and knowledge as a painter. The arrangement benefits both of them.

Case 3: This is the case of one of the "old-old," Mary, 87. A nutritionist by profession, Mary lives in a comfortable apartment in a retirement community. When she first arrived at Fairview Village in 1975, Mary wrote several professional papers in her field, and served on committees of organizations in her field. But today, the strain of getting to the nearby college library is too much for her. Now she contents herself with serving as an example to her Fairview neighbors. Each morning, in the hours before dawn, she makes ten "loops" through the

long, quiet corridors of her building. To keep her joints
limber and her legs strong, she also pedals a stationary
bicycle, on which she has logged several hundred miles.
She also eats a diet that she considers appropriate to her
age. Daily, she visits the village convalescent center.
There, she holds the frail hands of friends, chats with
them, and lets them know she cares.

These are just three examples of individual seniors
who are making good use of their knowledge and experience in their retirement years. Their stories could be
duplicated in most communities around the country, I
believe.

At this point, some of my readers may put up a hand
and say, "Wait a minute. In an earlier chapter you told me
to expand my horizons, try new things, be creative. Now
you are telling me to use the knowledge and experience
that I already have. Isn't that contradictory?" Answer:
No, it isn't. These two approaches to the retirement years
are not—or need not be—mutually exclusive. They can
exist side by side. A retired coach can use his knowledge
and experience to coach a little league team and still
acquire a new hobby, such as woodworking. After all, all
day, every day is yours to do with as you wish. You can
use your knowledge and experience for yourself and others; you can strike out into new and, for you, uncharted
areas of interest; or you can do both. The choice is yours.

We Are What We Think

The other day as I took a few minutes for quiet contemplation, various thoughts crossed my mind. One in
particular kept recurring. It related to the conversations I
had with psychiatrists with whom I was in association

during my years as director of mental health programming in Ohio. That thought was their emphasis on the power of the mind. "It's all in your mind" was not just a saying to these professionals; it was a fact of life and a part of their treatment approach. But long before the psychiatrists, this thought was expressed in the Bible. The King James rendering of Proverbs 23:7 reads: "As a man thinketh in his heart, so is he."

Interestingly, even Buddha, the renowned Indian religious leader, began his book entitled *The Dhammapada* with the following simple yet profound thought:

> We are what we think.
> All that we are arises with our thoughts.
> With our thoughts we make the world.

What do these words mean? What do they have to do with today's 65+ Generation?

Quite simply, Buddha and these others to whom I refer meant that the best—and the worst—that can happen to us lies within our power; that thought leads to action.

How does this apply to us, the New 65+ Generation? A 65+er may say, "Well, they've put me out to pasture; I'm a has-been, good for nothing." And so his thoughts come true. But many more will say, "I can write an essay, do physical things, paint a picture, put in a garden, make a quilt, give a speech about my experiences or my special knowledge, be active in my church, my club, my senior center, or in my community."

You can do these things, or think of other ones, because you have a vitality and a creativeness within you that only awaits your releasing it. *You are what you think!*

Grandma Moses did not say, "I can't paint." She said, "I used to paint some when I was younger and didn't have a family. I can do it again." And she did, simply, primitively, with her sincerity and detailed memories showing her the way. The end result was a blending of her knowledge, experience, and creativity.

But, none of us has to be a Grandma Moses, a Robert Frost, a Golda Meir. What if we don't become famous! We can be as good as we think we are, at least. One of the pleasures of my 20 years of association with 65+ers has been to see the talent shown in paintings by those who never before painted; or in stories and poems by those who have never before written; or in volunteer work by those who previously had never done for others.

And on a personal note, my mother-in-law at age 98 began painting with watercolors. Her pictures may not receive the attention of works by Grandma Moses but they are prized by those who have received them. She was still painting at the age of 102.

So use your experience and knowledge. And try creative new approaches to living. I cannot guarantee that doing so will give you longer life, though I believe it will contribute to that goal. I do guarantee you will find great joy and fulfillment in every day of your remaining years.

9

Don't Waste the Time You Have Left

"For from here on, it is your time that you are spending. And as you grow older you have less and less in your time bank account."

"Time is money."

Oh, how many times did you hear that said during your working life? It was repeated endlessly by supervisors, managers, and efficiency experts. It meant, of course, that you were to work more efficiently, be more productive so that the company might profit, to not waste time. And so, as a loyal employee, you lived by the maxim, "Time is money," hurrying ever faster through life.

But now that you are a member of the New 65+ Generation, you realize this aphorism must be rewritten. It should read: "Time is more precious than money." Now you must spend your time as carefully—perhaps more carefully—than you ever did the money you made in your wage-earning years. For, from here on, it is *your* time that you are spending. And as you grow older, you have less and less in your time bank account.

Time Is Distributed Evenly

Yet, isn't it interesting that time is the one ingredient of life each of us is given every day in equal measure? No matter whether rich or poor, genius or ordinary mortal, each of us begins the day with the same 24 hours to do with as we will. We may waste those hours or use them to the utmost, but the choice is ours. Our precious Declaration of Independence sets forth that "all men are created equal," but we know from experience that there are differences of intellect and talent among us. But with time there are no differences, for each of us is given by our Creator the same 24 hours.

Think how many times you've put off doing something until you "have more time"—that is, you think right then you don't have the time. What fools we are! The child walks dejectedly away with the book she wanted us to read to her—and a few months later she can read it for herself. Then there was the beautiful day on which we were too busy to go on a family picnic—but then comes another day when we offer to go, and it rains. Another time, a friend goes into the hospital for emergency surgery, but we let time slip by—and when we thought of it again, our friend was well and didn't need a solicitous visit. And then there are the wasted hours of regret—and they can really haunt you—stemming from the time you let days pass and didn't visit another sick friend, who unexpectedly left this life.

So many people and occasions are gone as our days are spent, particularly as we become members of the 65+ Generation. Yes, time has become more precious than money.

But don't waste time on regrets! And don't spend too much time looking back. Of course it's comforting and satisfying to recall former times. It's good to think about the past occasionally, because you can and should learn from it, but don't dwell on yesteryear too long. For then you find yourself living in the past and letting the years of your 65+ future slip away. You can fall into a nostalgic euphoria recalling the good times. Do that too long and too often and you're wasting your time. Time from now on is too precious to spend wantonly, dwelling on the past.

"The Brevity of Life"

Each of us has only so much time; no one knows how many days remain to us. That number varies among individuals for a variety of reasons. Some of those reasons are of our own making. But whatever factors come into play, eventually life comes to an end. When the Reverend Billy Graham made reference to his sixty-fifth birthday (see chapter entitled "Act Your Age"), he said that many people asked what he was thinking about on that auspicious occasion. His answer: "The brevity of life."

At 65+, we can understand the depth of emotion behind those few simple words. Yet we also know that at 65+ we represent the new generation—a generation that for the many who reach it promises years of new opportunities, new challenges.

Now that we are 65+ we have to use wisely the unknown period of time that is ours to spend as we will. We have to do the things we want to do—after we decide what those things are—not just follow the course set by others.

In my many years of working with older persons, it has been my observation that most do only a half-way job of planning for their retirement. In the months or even years preceding retirement, they think over and make conscious decisions about practical matters. For example: finances ("What will my income be? How much will I receive from Social Security, my pension, and from interest on my savings?"); living arrangements ("Stay in my present home, move to the Sun Belt, buy a condominium, or what?"); even preparations for death ("Is my insurance paid up? Is my will made? Do I have a grave plot? Are instructions written for my funeral? And where is the key to my safe deposit box?")

All these are important topics and it is laudable to make decisions concerning them. But once settled, and the retirement party behind you, what then? Then you are up against the second part of preparation for retirement: What to do with the rest of your life, with the 24 hours in each of the days ahead.

Retire to Something

Frankly, I think everyone should have a goal for his retirement years. Don't just retire *from* your job, but retire *to* something. You ought to have a goal, a purpose in life, something to get up for in the morning. It should be something you want to accomplish in those years, no matter how modest it may seem to others.

Now, as I explained in my introduction, this is not a how-to-do-it book on the retirement years. You will find several of those instructional works in your public library, complete with sources of information. Instead, let me here inject a case history—a true story—about one man who did an outstanding job of planning for his retirement. The reasons for presenting his story will be apparent as this chapter progresses.

Bill's Story

For a good share of his working life, J. W. "Bill" Cecil had been a carpenter and in the latter stages was co-owner of a hardware store in a small town. His working life provided all the skills and knowledge he needed to carry out his retirement plan.

He began his retirement preparations months before the actual event. He intended to set up a little woodworking shop, where he could turn out whatever he wanted, whenever he wanted, and at his own pace. He didn't plan to earn much money at this, just enjoy himself and benefit his customers.

He had a two-car garage behind his house that would be just the ticket. To house his car and various yard and garden implements, he constructed a one-and-a-half car addition to his garage. Scanning the classified section of his local newspaper, he found a small used gas furnace for sale and this he bought and installed. He also purchased a ceiling fan, which would help cool the shop in summer. Meanwhile, he let it be known among the visiting hardware salesmen that he was in the market for various machine tools. In due course he had a planer, machine drill, jigsaw and other implements. Most of the hand tools he already had. Of course, he would need wood. He dropped the word of what he needed to certain farmer customers and his friends at the lumberyard. Soon Bill had assembled a supply of kiln-dried lumber in the upstairs of his garage-turned-workshop. When the announced day of his retirement came, it was a relatively simple matter to move the last of his tools from the hardware store to his little workshop, and turn on the lights and the ventilating fan. He was in business.

Bill began making what he called a "little girl

dresser," a miniature bureau standing about 18 inches high. These he produced in walnut, cherry, and maple wood. Soon he couldn't keep up with the demand; and in the Christmas season, he worked harder and put in longer hours than he wanted to. But news of his skill and modest prices had spread. Throughout the years he had his little shop, this craftsman also found time to produce many custom items for people: grandfather clocks, dry sinks, a gun rack, stools, a schoolroom-style clock, a cradle.

What Bill set up could have become a good-sized business. But he didn't want that; he had no wish to produce only what would sell, hire workers, and eventually become a manager, complete with fancy office and a secretary. So he kept it small, worked the hours that suited him, and turned out the wood pieces he found satisfying to the eye and touch. Occasionally, he wanted a change, or he decided he'd been on his feet too much; so he'd just close the doors to his shop and he and his wife would take a trip.

"I didn't make much money from my retirement shop, but then I never intended to," Bill told me. "The letters and cards I received from people who appreciated my wood pieces, including one from the White House, was pay enough. Money wasn't my object; spreading joy to others was."

I call that a successful retirement. It's a fine example and I feel sure others have developed similar plans. The important thing is they are doing it.

Incidentally, his shop and the objects he produced there may give Bill a measure of immortality. Not only was he written up in various publications, he also signed each of his pieces and left in one of the drawers of each of the hundreds of dressers he sold a leaflet with his picture and a brief summary about himself.

"Get What You Like"

Bill's story brings to mind another maxim, one valuable enough to string a life on: "You'd better get what you like in life, because if you don't, you may be forced to like what you get."

That can apply to retirement, as well. I've met people who have gone into retirement communities who are dissatisfied because they are stuck playing cards, when they never really enjoyed card games; are attending dances in the entertainment room when they'd rather be out camping; people who feel they are forced to socialize when they prefer the solitary life; and others who like animals but, because of the rules of the community, are not able to keep any on the premises.

So what we all have to do, even before we retire, if possible, is to ponder what our choices are and how to achieve the lifestyle we want. We have to decide if we want a change, or whether we are perfectly happy and contented with things as they are.

It's Easy to Drift

Things as they are . . . . How easy it is to accept that approach. I can think of any number of retirees who drifted into a life of accepting each day as it comes. The retired administrator who took to walking a nearby shopping mall every afternoon to avoid his wife's endless TV soap operas. A journalist who vowed to read all the great books he'd put aside during his working life, but instead read only a few current mysteries. A plumber who sat with his wife and watched television game shows every day until they were cross-eyed. And a myriad of others who play golf, drink beer, visit, and watch TV almost every day.

For a long time I held the private theory that such a life could be fatal. But as time goes on, I see that many of the people who live these empty, uneventful existences, even the ones I have cited, can and do live into their 80s. For such people, it seems to me, retirement is just a means of existing, in a pleasant, comfortable style, perhaps, but still no more than existing.

The best retirements, it seems to me, are planned or evolved by people with the most active minds, who aren't satisfied with things as they are. People like my wood craftsman friend, Bill; or Jim McGavran, who began in his late 60s to write a column titled "Perspectives" for his local newspaper. Then there was Anna Nord, the widow of a minister, who wanted to keep busy and help her family and church as much as possible. To that end, she was constantly sewing for her grandchildren, the church mission, and herself; did baking and canning, again for her family, friends, and neighbors. Into the bargain, she added beauty to her world via her extensive flower and vegetable gardens.

To my mind, these people didn't waste the time they had left.

Now, as I have often said in this book, we are all different; each of us is an individual. Thus, not everyone can be the forward-thinking, planning individual who can create a life plan for his or her retirement years. For some, it comes as a natural evolution, as I believe it did for Anna Nord, rising naturally out of her Christian philosophy. For others, it may be enough to establish short-term retirement goals, planning no more than a year ahead. One person may say, "This year, I'm going to read a book a month." If his eyesight is not what it used to be, he may choose the large-print editions or taped books, of which there is now a generous supply. Another may say, "I'm going to fix up our house this year, starting with a paint job on the bedrooms." Others may decide to learn a language; read the Bible; or take up golf, bird-watching, or gardening.

Choose Something

Whichever you choose, choose something. *Don't waste the time you have left.*

It surprises me sometimes to learn how early many people retire these days. Many are no more than 55 or so. After the "honeymoon period" of retirement is over, a number of them wake up one morning and say to themselves, "This is boring, I've got to do *something.*" Being used to working every day, they go looking for part-time jobs. Some miss the stimulation of work and the social involvement. Some need the money to supplement their income; others just like having the extra spending money. For anyone over 50, finding a part-time job is no easy task, but possible. Most retirees have marketable skills and they may live in a community that has a job placement bureau for older persons.

Not only are these part-time retirees making good use of the time they have left, they may actually be saving their lives. As my friend, the late Julian Marcus, founder of the Julian Marcus Senior Citizens Placement Center in Columbus, Ohio, once said, "When seniors are challenged, they tend to live longer." In fact, the suicide rate for those who retire is twelve times higher than for those who go back to work.

Facing Your Fears

Now, granted, none of what I suggest in this chapter is easy. It takes courage and energy to lead an active life. There are no easy ruts that lead to happiness. I have heard stories of old people who, fearing attacks by young hoodlums, have not been out of their homes for months. Incredible! True, these elderly people may live in slums of large cities, so have reason to be terror-stricken. But perhaps others read these same stories and are afflicted with the same dreads, yet live in decent neighborhoods where they need have no such fears.

So, too, do many seniors fear loneliness. To be sure, loneliness can incapacitate older persons, keeping them from making the most of their retirement years. But I wonder if some of the fault isn't theirs. One elderly woman of my acquaintance often complained of being lonely, yet she lived within a short walking distance of Kingwood Center in Mansfield, Ohio, one of the finest horticulture centers in America. There is always something new to see or do at Kingwood, and it has a library of horticulture books and magazines second to none. I could only conclude this woman wanted to be lonely.

Another woman told her daughter-in-law that she was often lonely. The daughter-in-law, a very resourceful young woman, suggested, "Why don't you bake one of your famous pies tomorrow morning, then call some of your neighbors to come over for pie and coffee? Or have a different neighbor in each morning?" The woman did none of these things. Perhaps she wanted to be bored and lonely. Perhaps she was more lazy and/or timid than she was bored. The first step toward overcoming boredom is the desire to be active.

You're Never Too Old

Reading some of the foregoing retirement success stories, such as those about Bill Cecil or Anna Nord, a reader may conclude, "Well, that's all very well for them, but I'm 75 years old. I'm just too old for that." Nonsense! To put it in the modern vernacular, that's just a cop out. It's never too late to start living a successful retirement life. Recently I read a magazine article about a 76-year-old retired accountant who took up investing as a "hobby." Through his skill he built a $500,000 stock portfolio, ensuring that he and his wife will spend the rest of their lives free from financial worries. This man didn't lament, "My life is over. I'll never be rich now." Instead, he just went ahead and did it. If you think that man is unusual, you're forgetting Colonel Sanders, who was actually drawing Social Security checks when he started his famous Kentucky Fried Chicken chain of restaurants.

Does all this mean that you should go back to keeping a schedule, filling your day with frenzied hours of activities the way you used to? Not at all. There is an old Chinese proverb that says, "Hurry slowly, and you soon arrive." That saying comes from Jean Hersey's wonderful little book, *Gardening and Being*. A retiree herself, Hersey suggests taking time to cherish life. "Life is lovely to savor," she writes. "When you ruminate or contemplate or savor your day, you are nourishing the spirit."[1]

So don't waste the time you have left. But take time to nourish the spirit. I think that's what Andy Rooney, the syndicated newspaper columnist, had in mind when he wrote:

"Money shouldn't be saved for a rainy day. It should be saved and spent for a beautiful day."

10

Act Your Age . . . . Most of the Time

"What do we mean, exactly, when we admonish someone to 'act your age'?"

$\mathbf{M}$ina and Joe, a retired couple in their 70s, have finished their evening meal and are having coffee and watching the evening news on television. Abruptly appearing on the screen is an action scene on a baseball diamond peopled by elderly men.

It develops that this is a group of 65+ men who have retired to Florida. To put some excitement into their lives they have organized a softball team. They seem to be having a wonderful time. True, the batter's swing is a trifle slow, but no matter, the pitch is no speed ball, either. When they run for the bases, the runners puff a bit, but they get there, sometimes before the throw.

"Hey, that looks like fun," exclaims Joe. Mina purses her lips and says nothing.

Anyone watching that television news-feature might

have thought nine innings under the Florida sun could be rather hazardous for those old fellows. But on the contrary, they appear exceptionally healthy for their ages. And most of all, they seem to be having a perfectly marvelous time.

In the final scene an elderly batter swats one into the infield, slides into first base in a cloud of dust. The first baseman stretches for the throw. "Yur out!" the umpire bellows.

"Hurumph!" snorts Mina. "The old fools . . . why don't they act their age!"

Later in the evening, Mina tunes in on one of her favorite programs, a country-western show. There is a barn dance in progress, with men in plaid shirts and overalls fiddling and a group of older women in bonnets and swirling skirts square dancing. Most of the women are gray- or even white-haired, but they seem to be having a wonderful time.

"Hurumph!" Joe grouses to himself. "The old fools . . . why don't they act their age?" But as Mina is smiling and toe-tapping to the music, he thinks it better to say these things to himself.

"Act Your Age"

Let us leave Mina and Joe to their television watching, and talk about that well-known catch phrase, "Act your age." It can be a slippery expression at any age, but particularly so when you are 65+.

What do we mean, exactly, when we admonish someone to "Act your age"? Is it desirable or undesirable to "act your age"? And what is your age? Is it your chronological age—that is, the age indicated by your birth certificate? Or is it the age you feel? That age, of course, can vary from day to day, even hour to hour. Or is it your biological age—the number your doctor may offer after examining you?

To my thinking, the first important mental exercise is to put away the chronological absolute from your mind. But then, you've already done that, haven't you? When you walk past a plate glass store window and view your reflection, you don't really like what you see, do you? That's not the real you, the person that's inside and looking out of your eyes, is it? No, the real you is not as old as that person gazing back at you from the window. You now realize that wasn't just a funny joke when Jack Benny always gave his age as 39—we all laughed because we understood and felt the same way. Incidentally, to show you how far we've come in longevity, evangelist Billy Graham in a recent television sermon stated that he stopped referring to his chronological age when he reached 65. He, too, is 65+—but who's counting?

Old Is How You Look at It

Curiously, most of us lose track of our age from time to time, either unthinkingly or on purpose. My mother-in-law, who at 102, occasionally commented about some "old" woman of 75; and when reminded that she was a lot older than that, she was wide-eyed with disbelief. That's how most older persons feel unless their health goes or a bone breaks. Then you are as old as you feel!

Over the years, I've talked with many people of different ages and walks of life and have noted that, without exception, children don't think of themselves as being in their 30s some day; people in their 30s don't really believe they will be middle-aged; nor do the middle-aged dwell on the thought that they, too, might be 65 some day. I say "might be" because not everyone in a high school graduation class will survive to age 65.

For reasons not for us to question, the Creator did not put that anxious awareness of our individual mortality in our make-up in our day-to-day living. Evidently the Creator wanted us to be cheerful. We are to furiously expend energy while growing; cheerfully work and play hard; tear around noisily and productively, reaching out for what we want to achieve. But it appears we aren't "programmed" to visualize our own old age and demise.

An extreme example of this came to my attention a few years ago. For some 20 years, the annual Ohio State Fair included special programs for senior citizens, offering a wide variety of activities. In the earlier years we even had cookie bake-offs and square-dancing in the 100-degree August heat. (Incidentally, we always had a nurse in attendance, but the only people who keeled over were teenagers, never a senior citizen.) Well, in one of our two tents, we'd serve tea or coffee and cookies from the bake-off before the buses left to transport the seniors back to their home communities. That particular summer, we asked the wives of state officials to serve as hostesses. The next day, one of the wives became hysterical and suffered a nervous breakdown lasting for several weeks, because she had suddenly become aware that "someday I'm going to be like that."

"Like what?"

"*Old*—and grabbing cookies to put in my pocket, and wrinkles . . ."

Unseen by her, she already had some lines of age

(she was in her 40s), but mentally she was still in her early 20s and the belle-of-the-ball.

That's an outsize illustration of the reluctance people feel about facing the reality of aging. It underscores the fact that the negative image of tottering old people and the false myth of mind-loss perpetuated through the years by the media and in cartoons do frighten people. Now, at 65+, there need be nothing to frighten us. It's time to rejoice! We've been blessed—we're alive and 65, or older!

"Accept Your Age"

Rather than telling each other to "Act your age," we should be saying, "Accept your age." Live your life to the fullest and make of it what you will. It is not just "old age," but a later chapter in the book called Life. Having come this far, you should be happy and shout, "Hallelujah! I've made it this far. Now I'm going on to do it my way."

But accepting your age doesn't mean you have to conduct yourself in the ways the public seems to think a person 65 or 75 should act. Even today, too many older people appear to believe they should dress the way their grandparents did, in somber, conservative clothes; should sit quietly in their chairs with hands folded, so as not to be noticed. Others just sit down and say to their families, "Take care of me. I've earned it." If you do these things, you're just falling into the stereotype that some seniors and much of the public have of older people. For goodness sake, don't add to our image problem!

This is all very well for you and me, but what of Mina and Joe, the televiewers we met in the beginning of this chapter? The couple was very concerned about what is appropriate action for individuals at their ages. I wish Joe and Mina could have listened in on a discussion I recently had with an intelligent woman of my acquaintance. Although not yet a senior citizen, she summarized the matter in one sentence:

"Act your age with dignity and intelligence, but never forget the child within you."

Supposing we take up the first part of the sentence: "Act your age with dignity and intelligence." This suggests that there are occasions when "Act your age!" is good advice. For example:

When doing physical activities. For instance, it's okay to play tennis if you're 65+, but don't do it in the hot sun. Wait until the sun goes down, and drink plenty of liquids and take frequent rests. Pace yourself and use good common sense when doing other physical things, such as mowing the lawn, gardening, or exercising. And if you've never before done a particular physical activity, doctor and spouse willing, ease into it slowly, allowing your body to adjust.

When behind the wheel. Perhaps nowhere is it more important that a senior citizen act his or her age than when behind the steering wheel of a car. It's a time to be honest with yourself about physical shortcomings—weak eyesight, poor hearing, slow reflexes. Take remedial action if possible; if not, you may want to garage your car and take a bus or taxi. Or perhaps you have shrunk up somewhat in size and can't see over the steering wheel anymore. Pillows on the seat or extenders on the pedals may help.

Naturally, you'll want to be guided by your doctor concerning your capacity to drive. But don't wait for your doctor to tell you. I believe most seniors know when they are no longer capable of safe driving, particularly on freeways or in busy commercial areas. If you come to that realization, determine to drive a car only on familiar streets in your town or neighborhood. If in doubt, for your safety and that of others, don't drive at all.

Perhaps this is a good time to emulate Billy Graham and forget your chronological age. Better to be guided by your biological age. According to your birth records, you may be, say, 71. But your doctor examines you and says, "You have the heart of a man of 40 or 45." Another senior may have a physical and be told that "because of your sedentary life, your arteries are those of a person of 88." Under such circumstances, it's better to listen to your doctor and forget Jack Benny and his "I'm 39."

When feeling frisky. "You're as young as you feel" could prove a dangerous saying. A man of 75 may be feeling pretty frisky. Frisky enough that he starts chasing the girls of 25. He divorces his wife, buys a set of "zooty threads," as he calls them, and a zippy convertible, and has himself a big time in Las Vegas. But when the money's gone, he has a headache and an upset stomach, some duds he will look funny in back home, and not much else. "Act your age" would be a better saying for this man.

In dress. Must oldsters dress like oldsters? Must men over 65 dress only in dark suits or coat sweaters and gray trousers? Must the women always be garbed in flowered jersey dresses and Cuban heels? Not at all. I love to see 65+ women in the modern, colorful pants suits; the men in sport coats and slacks. On the other hand, I feel like shouting "Act your age!" when I see an older woman in a teenager's short skirt, or her hair done up in Shirley Temple ringlets. Somewhere there is a middle ground between the traditional old people's clothes and the brash clothes of the young. Based on my observations, most of our seniors are finding that middle ground.

"The Child Within"

Now let me take up the second part of my friend's sentence: ". . . never forget the child within you."

Obviously my friend believes that, no matter what your age, there is buried inside you the child you once were. Now, Dr. Ashley Montagu, author and noted anthropologist, writes in his book *Growing Young* that as we grow older, certain traits we had as children are gradually lost or abandoned. He lists these traits as:

Curiosity
Open-mindedness
Eagerness to learn
Willingness to experiment
Imagination
Humor
Need to love[1]

My friend agrees these traits sometimes do fade in many people. But she is convinced the child is present even in the most dignified individuals; that child is just submerged deeper in some people than in others. (Who can forget old Ebenezer Scrooge in Charles Dickens' immortal *A Christmas Carol*?[2] Even in Scrooge the child was alive, though it took the Spirit of Christmas Past to resurrect him.) As we grow older, we have to make a conscious effort to let that child in us emerge.

Says my friend, rather adamantly: "When I'm old, if I want to go out and fly a kite in the spring, I'm going to do it. And wear shorts into the bargain." On the other hand, she wouldn't wear those shorts to the supermarket, for instance. Nor does she plan to wear miniskirts, exposing varicose veins (if any), or wear her hair like a teenager. But she's not going to wear long dresses and cluck her tongue at everything the young do, either. Besides kite-flying, my friend mentioned a number of other activities that might call on the child within you, such as bicycling, playing volleyball, shooting baskets, playing tennis, or bowling.

Author May Sarton in *The House by the Sea* twice refers to the child within us. The first reference appears in a letter from a Chilean friend, Eugenia, a psychotherapist, who writes: ". . . I am sure we have taken you for granted more than once, forgetting that in the artist the child is alive and has to be . . . ."

Interestingly, I have noticed this very quality in the many artists whom I have met over the years. They say things like, "Let's play with that idea for a while and see what happens." Again, an artist may begin a project in a spirit of fun and the resulting painting or sculpture takes on a playful air that makes it appealing to the viewer. Grandma Moses, I like to believe, began the paintings of her old age in a spirit of enjoyment and adventure. To become a child again is to shuck off all sophisticated, worldly ideas, ideals, and cares: to return to true innocence.

Sarton reveals a slightly different meaning of "childlike" in this second quotation from the same book: ". . . The child in the old person is a precious part of his being able to handle the slow imprisonment. As he is able to do less, he enjoys everything in the present, with a childlike enjoyment. It is a saving grace, and I see it when Judy is with me here."[3]

(Judy, I should mention, is a friend who has become senile.)

Of Grandfathers and Grandchildren

I have always held a private theory that this is one reason grandparents, particularly grandfathers, get along so well with their grandchildren. The grandfather returns to that childlike innocence that he left behind so long ago. But at 65+ it is acceptable to let the child in you come to the surface. Thus a grandfather (or grandmother) can, without loss of dignity, ride a bike, play catch, gather nuts in the fall, ride a carousel, fly a kite, tell ghost stories, go to the zoo and/or circus, build a model car or airplane—or do whatever you and your grandchild choose.

So, as you can see, the phrase "Act your age" is not so simple and clear-cut as it first appears. Yet it bears being repeated, for regardless of how we may see ourselves within ourselves, we cannot escape the biological time clock. And why should we? Each period of life offers its own distinctive opportunities. There are opportunities, challenges, and choices for those of us 65+ equal to those of any age.

Life is to be lived regardless of your age. Each age period is precious and the most precious is the one that follows after age 65. This is because at earlier age periods most of us perceived ourselves at whatever our chronological age might have been. But at age 65+ you perceive yourself as younger than you actually are.

So now we can pause and look around to find our real niche. Let's decide what age we want to be and discover what we really can do ourselves to be of benefit and help to others, if that is our inclination.

We can warm others with our sincere affection; become interested in a new sport or craft; be as interested in and as loving with our spouse as when we were first married; be cheerful and give a big smile to every older person we see, especially those with frowns and sad faces—for they need to see us 65+ers "act our age."

11

You Have Power and Influence—Use Them

"You are a powerful person, if you exercise the power you have."

I̲n Ecclesiastes 3:1–4, we are told:

> There is a time for everything, and a season for every activity under heaven:
> A time to be born and a time to die; a time to plant and a time to uproot,
> A time to kill and a time to heal; a time to tear down and a time to build,
> A time to weep and a time to laugh; a time to mourn and a time to dance . . .

What do these verses have to do with power and influence and why am I quoting them? In these verses the author of Ecclesiastes is telling us that God provides a time for everything. As members of the New 65+

Generation, you and I are reminded it is time for us to use the power and influence that we possess.

Senior Power

First, let's talk about senior power—the strength that we older Americans possess collectively and can wield in the political sphere. Then we'll consider the influence for good that each of us has as individuals.

You don't have to be 65+ to know that we have senior power. Who has not heard of Maggie Kuhn and her Gray Panthers and such organizations as the American Association of Retired Persons and the National Council of Senior Citizens? They, as well as others, are listened to by our local, state, and national officials. It is because of these collective efforts that Social Security benefits have been protected from the cuts periodically proposed. And think of what could happen to Medicare and other important programs brought into existence in fulfillment of the promise made to older persons in the Older American Act, were it not for these groups.

Indeed, it is through our political process that seniors all over the country receive reduced rates for many goods and services, including bus and airline fares. Through senior power, in many states, we now enjoy lower property taxes and utility bills. Because of our need—and our voting power—the elderly poor have been aided by the government in obtaining decent housing.

As a 65+er, you may have more power than you realize. Although seniors represent approximately 12 percent of the population, a higher percentage of us vote in national elections than most of the other age groups, as studies have clearly shown. No wonder politicians listen to us. Paradoxically, the reason for our voting record is that we have the time to devote to study of the issues, both individually and in study groups. Then we do take the time to go and vote. But more importantly, most of us agree very strongly with a sentiment expressed by the late Nelson Cruikshank, who served as White House Counselor on Aging and President of the National Council of Senior Citizens. He said it is through the ballot that we assure the perpetuation of freedom and liberty.

(By the way, let us be sure to use that power wisely and well. Let us not selfishly say, "We're only in favor of those issues that will better our lot." By that reasoning, we would vote down school levies, for example, arguing that "we don't have children in school anymore. Why should we pay to educate someone else's kids?" Rather, we should consider what is best for our families, friends, and for future generations.)

Influence for Good

But perhaps equal to—or even greater than—our collective power is our influence for good as individuals. Ever the optimist, I believe there is in each of us a measure of altruism that helps fulfill our desire to live a more meaningful life. The opportunity to do something about that spark of altruism is never better than when you join the 65+ Generation.

As individuals, living in our neighborhoods and communities, we may have more influence for good than many political leaders, religious teachers, and others. Why not? There are literally millions of us. And no matter what our physical shortcomings, most of us have the time and should have the motivation. As 65+ers, we know that the years ahead are bound to be fewer than those behind, and so we must use that time to add meaning to the lives of others.

A few years ago a survey was taken of a large number of senior citizens, asking "How would you meet difficult times?" To their credit, the majority said that adversity could be defeated by "sharing, kindness, courtesy, and love." Individually, we of the new generation *can* make a difference! All we need to do is to put into practice the beliefs of the majority of that survey.

No matter what your status in life, no matter where you may be, you can bring about change. Think of what it might mean if you and I, and every 65+er, would reflect sharing, kindness, courtesy, and love in our actions. What an example we would be setting!

Bill's Story

It occurs to me that these four qualities can best be summed up in the word "neighborliness." Let me tell you about a man who, in my view, is the personification of small-town good neighborliness. A carpenter and later hardware merchant during his working life, Bill has used his retirement years to extend the good-neighbor policy that once occupied his Sundays. Although 90, he puts in a big garden each year and keeps his neighbors in green beans, tomatoes, corn, and other vegetables. Naturally, these are gifts; he never accepts a penny for them.

In winter, Bill clears snow from the sidewalks of elderly persons who live nearby. For employed neighbors who must leave their cars outdoors, he will clean their windshields of ice and snow on winter mornings. At any time of the year, he will do errands for people in need, or drive a friend or neighbor—of any age—to the doctor or dentist. As a friend said of him, "Bill never says no to anyone. He doesn't know the meaning of the word."

Another man we knew would take grocery orders from the women who lived in his senior community and shop for them. This is the same man who let my wife go ahead of him in the supermarket line, saying: "Go ahead. I know you're in a hurry and I have plenty of time." (This was especially appreciated, since at his age and state of health he did not have that much time left.)

All of us, I would imagine, love our grandchildren. We shower them with gifts, set up bank accounts or trust funds for them, take them to circuses and fairs. One woman of my acquaintance did more: She became aware that her grown daughter was so busy with her clubs and committees that she failed to notice her youngest child was doing poorly in school. The grandmother said to herself, "If this child doesn't get some help, she'll fail." So she asked to keep the girl for a while and gave her the tutoring she needed. Basking in her grandmother's love and attention, the child responded and did pass. Doubtless this is a story that can be duplicated by others in the New 65+ Generation. Time is a gift the elderly have to give.

This same woman formed a group to sew for the poor. One afternoon a week the women would bring a sack lunch, socialize, and stitch. The clothes they made and repaired were distributed to the needy through a local church. Later, in her eighties, when circulatory problems restricted this woman's mobility, she sold her small home and moved into a senior citizens apartment complex. But she did not become a television addict.

When a program was to take place in the community center, it was she who went around and solicited her neighbors to attend. "It will do you good to get out," she would prod.

Spreading Joy

The opportunity to spread some joy may turn up when you least expect it. One such occasion came on a chill, overcast spring day when I was patronizing a small downtown peanut shop. It is a wonderful store, redolent of the smell of nuts of every kind, from expensive cashews to peanuts in the shell. As an elderly man stood gazing over the brimming trays of nuts in the display cases, a young salesgirl came up behind the case where he stood.

"What would you like?" she asked. But she was frowning and gazing out the shop's front window as she said it.

"Why are you so unhappy-looking?" the elderly gentleman inquired, setting aside her offer of help.

The girl, looking even more bleak, replied impatiently, "Well, just look how ugly it is outside. And besides, I have to work today."

The elderly gentleman smiled and replied, "Young woman, I am 78 years old and when you're my age, every day is a wonderful day, particularly when you consider the alternative."

He bought a sack of peanuts and left the store. It is my belief he ate those peanuts with great enjoyment, and doubtless shared them with others.

Perhaps later that day or weeks or even years afterwards the girl may have recalled his words.

Now, let me readily concede that such actions may not come easily to some of us. Reaching 65+ does not result in a miraculous change in the individual. But each of us can try. One rather high-class woman told me, "I don't much care for a woman who lives downstairs in my apartment building, but I share my newspaper with her. I know she doesn't have much money to spare, and she appreciates the paper." Think of the many seniors who could make a difference in the lives of others through such a simple gesture. And the recipients of your bounties need not be seniors; they can be people of any age.

But, you insist, "I am not a do-gooder; I couldn't do anything like that. I don't go around telling people to 'Have a nice day!' and drawing happy faces on the bottom of my letters." Others may also demur, saying, "I just don't find it in my nature to tell other people how to live."

"I Changed the Way I Thought"

To those people I would urge a reading of an essay entitled "A Light in the Toolbox" by Richard Bach, the man who wrote *Jonathan Livingston Seagull.* "A Light in the Toolbox" appears in Bach's wonderful collection of essays, *A Gift of Wings.* Bach, as you may know, is an experienced airplane pilot; but for years he insisted, "I'm no mechanic. Why," he said, "I don't even know which end of the screwdriver to hit the nail with." Then one day, he bought a "crazy old biplane," as he called it, a craft seemingly with a mind of its own. Certainly it was a plane that would conk out at odd times and leave him stranded in the middle of a farmer's pasture in July. The result was that Bach had to take another look at himself:

"That was how the rarest event in life came to me . . . I changed the way I thought," Bach writes. "I learned the mechanics of airplanes."[1]

Think of it: "I changed the way I thought." Most adults don't even think that's possible. But Bach shows in this personal experience essay that, by making a conscious decision to change, many things are possible. "I can't paint," says a senior citizen. And so you cannot paint. "I couldn't possibly walk a mile," says another. And so he cannot walk a mile. But to the individuals who change the way they think, painting a picture, walking a mile, or doing whatever they choose is possible.

How should you begin to assert the "new you"? First, smile! This will have an effect on those upon whom you smile and on you. How about a cheerful good morning, good afternoon, or good evening greeting to those you meet? And when was the last time you complimented anyone? Suppose you tried these simple exercises on members of your family, on your friends. Do you think it would have an effect? Of course it would. Multiply these actions by everyone in the New 65+ Generation and you will realize how successful we would be in bringing about change.

The Gift of Yourself

The beauty of all this is that it won't cost you a penny. Think of it: bringing about change without it costing a cent. Now, of course, there would be a cost. The cost of your personal transformation. It isn't easy to force yourself to do something that you don't usually do. It isn't easy to continue doing so when you're rebuffed by those you seek to help or influence.

Perhaps that is why these lines from *The Prophet* by the Lebanese-American poet Kahlil Gibran are so true:

You give but little when you give your possessions.
It is when you give of yourself that you truly give.[2]

The hardest thing to give is of yourself. That's why *you* are important. You are a powerful person if you exercise the power that you have. You can bring about the kind of world that our Judeo-Christian heritage envisions.

You will remember that, according to St. John at the Last Supper, Jesus said, "A new command I give you: Love one another. As I have loved you, so you must love one another" (13:34). That charge was given to the apostles, but it applies to each of us. The apostles were not powerful, wealthy, or exceptionally learned. They were ordinary men with little to single them out for the extraordinary service they would perform.

Members of today's clergy, regardless of faith or denomination, are the direct descendants of the apostles, but they alone cannot fulfill the charge from Jesus.

Sharing, kindness, courtesy, and love—these human qualities shine through all the actions of the people I have cited in this chapter. By bringing these traits into play, these people did make a difference. Anyone 65+ can do the same.

12

Don't Overlook the Magic within You

"To live is to function."

"When we retire, we have two choices," my friend Walter explained to me. "One is to lie back and say, 'I've worked 45 or 50 years for this—now it's up to someone else to take care of me. I've got it coming.'"

But there is another way, elucidated Walter, an active, excited-about-life 70-year-old. "The other choice is to say: 'I'm going to be responsible for my life from here on out, just as I always have. No lying back and being waited on for me!'"

Sometimes it does seem that society and in some cases our families are going to get together and take care of us retirees. Our children, grown now, take an interest in our living situation, finances, and health. As to society, it has conferred many benefits on today's 65+ers over the past two decades—higher Social Security checks, Medicare, discount cards, special travel rates, lower property taxes, reduced utility bills. And for many, these boons were, and still are, needed. In all too many cases, they make the difference between living decently and living in want.

"Aging Is a State of Mind"

But if we're voting, I'm casting my ballot for Walter, who said, "I'm going to be responsible for my life from here on out, just as I always have." Now, it's easy to say, "Walter is one kind of person, but I'm another." But is that entirely true? Of course, we're all different, but aging is a state of mind as well as a physical process. So each of us must start with the belief—the conviction— that we are responsible for ourselves and will continue to be until the end.

All through life we are told about our responsibilities and, so, when we reach 65, we can't wait to take it easy; we look forward to nothing to do—no responsibilities. It's a dream we carry with us from the time we begin working—waiting for that time "when I can say good-bye to my days of drudgery and move into the world of my dreams." But when you launch into that new life, you discover you do have responsibilities. My dictionary says the word *responsible* means: "answerable or accountable, as for something within one's power, control, or management (often followed by *to* or *for*)." So we are accountable for our own lives and well-being, our happiness and that of others; and we are answerable to ourselves, our families, friends, and neighbors—and to our God.

Now, during my many years as Director of the Ohio Commission on Aging, I often asked groups of senior citizens, "Do you feel you have responsibilities?" The general feeling of an overwhelming number of these 65+ individuals was, "Of course we have responsibilities. We shouldn't sit around on our duffs," they said. Others said, "We should share whatever experience and knowledge we have. It may not be much, but it might help someone." Many ended their comments by asking: "But how do we go about it?"

The answer, it seems to me, breaks down into two parts. We have individual responsibilities and collective responsibilities. Let's look at the individual ones first.

Individual Responsibilities

Perhaps the major thought I have to leave with you in this section really comes from Justice Oliver Wendell Holmes, whom you met in a previous chapter. At one point in his lengthy career, Justice Holmes was asked to define the meaning of life. After considerable soul-searching, he offered this simple definition: "To live is to function."

To Live Is to Function.

By this, I believe the great jurist meant not to retire to apathy, to the trivia of living, to idleness, to vegetation—but to function. In the case of the senior citizen, at a less demanding pace, with less furor, but, nonetheless, to function. All through your working life, you had to function. You may not always have enjoyed what you were doing, but you did it. Why? Because you were a responsible person. Now that you're 65+, your goal should be similar: not just to live—but to function. And "to function" means to keep busy, to do something satisfying, not just for yourself but for others. Many of us now

65+ have laid such a course all through our lives and we know that the personal gain from doing so far exceeds the effort it takes.

Now let me suggest a number of ways for you to function and thereby perform as a responsible 65+er:

Help others. It seems elementary to state this, but we do indeed have a responsibility to help others. Even small services may mean a lot: going to the library for a friend or neighbor, or running some similar errand; taking a friend for a ride, particularly someone who's been shut in; writing a letter for a senior citizen who is ill or whose handwriting has grown too "trembly"; just visiting or being company for someone who's lonely. In short, be a good friend and/or neighbor. Do these small services in keeping with Jesus' admonishment, as noted in Lloyd Douglas's classic book, *Magnificent Obsession.* As recorded in the Book of Matthew (6:1–4), Jesus in his Sermon on the Mount urged:

> Be careful not to do your "acts of righteousness" before men, to be seen by them. If you do, you will have no reward from your Father in heaven.
>
> So when you give to the needy, do not announce it with trumpets, as the hypocrites do in the synagogues and on the streets, to be honored by men. I tell you the truth, they have received their reward in full. But when you give to the needy, do not let your left hand know what your right hand is doing, so that your giving may be in secret. Then your Father, who sees what is done in secret, will reward you.

Helping others can also include visiting friends, neighbors, or relatives when they are hospitalized or in a nursing home. One day, while walking in a small town, I spotted the following words painted in large letters on the porch awning of a nursing home:

LOVE IS AGELESS
VISIT US

The sign speaks for itself, doesn't it?

Set a good example for other 65+ citizens. Remember, the public already has a stereotyped view of the senior citizen; don't do anything that will confirm that view (see chapter entitled "Myths and Misconceptions"). On the contrary, as an exemplar of your generation, set a good example in dress, attitude, comportment, health and social habits, manners, and the like.

Just holding the hand of a person who is ill or in a coma may be the kindest thing you could do. Very much to the point is an experience told to me by a friend, who had gone into the hospital for cataract surgery. At the appointed hour he was wheeled into the operating room. He'd had various shots while still in his room, and he was pretty well under the anesthetic. The surgeons and nurses surrounded him, and although he knew the surgery had a high rate of success, his apprehension mounted. Presently he felt someone take his hand. "It was the most incredibly reassuring feeling," my friend told me.

But let my friend continue the story: "I said, 'Nurse?' just to affirm her presence. 'Yes,' she replied, 'this is the nurse. Just go to sleep now.' And I felt the doctor start to administer the local anesthetic. And then I wafted off into unconsciousness." Not until the next day did my friend recall the incident. "By then it was too late to find out who the nurse was and thank her. I never saw her face. It was a simple act, her holding my hand, just for a few moments and right at that critical time; but I will always remember it," he said.

Perhaps you are one of those who hates to visit the old and sick, the lonely, or the dying. But, based on this story, I believe that the simple act of sitting with someone, of saying a kind word, or holding a hand for a few minutes may mean more than you can ever imagine.

Don't complain. Particularly, don't fall in love with your afflictions. Actor and entertainer Mickey Rooney, speaking at the Ohio Governor's Conference on Aging in 1978, pointed out that many seniors get possessive about their infirmities. "My arthritis, my gall bladder," they say. "Nobody dares take it away from them, you know. That's '*my* arthritis,'" Rooney mocked. His antidote: to remember that "age is an attitude."

Smile and have a kind word for everyone. Dr. Frank Prout, when he was president of Bowling Green (Ohio) State University in the 1940s, made it a practice to smile and speak to every student he passed on campus. His custom inspired the students: they found themselves smiling and speaking to everyone, too. It was a wonderful place to go to school, an alumnus of that period told me.

Be a good citizen. Study the issues; keep up on today's problems as well as senior citizen issues. And *vote.* (More about this in the chapter "You Have Power and Influence—Use Them.")

Preserve the past. Many people keep advising senior citizens to "Forget the past. It's gone! Set your eyes on the future." Well, fine. But memories keep crowding in, don't they? As we get older, due to some phenomenon of the brain cells, I suppose, the days we spent in grade school become more vivid than what we had for breakfast that morning. My solution is not to attempt to banish the past, but to retain it in some way, preferably permanently.

There are several ways to do this. One I call my Federalist Papers approach. The Federalist Papers, you recall, were a series of essays written by Alexander Hamilton, James Madison, and John Jay and published anonymously in 1787–88 to explain to the American public the Federal Constitution. Like Publius (the trio's pen name) you might write out some of your thoughts and memories, perhaps in a series of letters to your children or grandchildren. (True, you may talk with your children each week by phone, but seldom do these conversations deal with memories, deep feelings, or important ideas.) The letters can then be bound into a notebook, which can be handed down from generation to generation. Perhaps this will lead one of your children or grandchildren to do the same for his or her offspring. An alternate idea might be to tape-record some of your memories on various topics. This has the bonus of preserving your voice for your posterity. Now that VCRs are common, consider doing a videotaped interview in which you reminisce about your childhood, family memories, and so on.

But perhaps you're not the articulate type. Your assignment can be to find all the family pictures, date them, and identify the individuals in them. You can't imagine how important this can be to an heir left with a pile of pictures he or she can't identify. Another thing: If you have a family Bible, bring it up to date.

Make new friends, including some younger ones. One way to stay involved in life is to make new friends. Don't be like an 85-year-old friend of mine who looked around him in church one day and realized he didn't see anyone he knew. "It hit me like a thump on the head that all my friends were either dead or in nursing homes— and all these younger people were strangers to me." As poet, novelist and essayist May Sarton writes in *The House by the Sea: A Journal*, ". . . the basic pattern of life changes radically when there is no one left, for instance, who remembers one as a child. Each such death is an earthquake that buries a little more of the past forever."

Keep an open mind to new ideas. Now, of course, if you have been awake during the last half-century or so, you naturally have convictions. And it is good to have ideas and ideals you believe in. Nevertheless, as you age, it's important to talk a bit less and listen a lot more. Listening attentively is a sign of an open mind.

Stay healthy. (See chapters "Good Health Is Found in Motion" and "Be Alive to Stay Alive.")

Do for yourself as much as possible. Some oldsters, when ill, or simply as they age, want to be taken care of hand and foot. Others are like Florida Scott-Maxwell, author of *The Measure of My Days*, who in her 80s was obliged to submit to a more-or-less major operation. Several days after the surgery, she was permitted to take a bath in a tub; and while doing so, she confessed to the nurse that being ill had made her bad-tempered and want to say, "Let me alone, I'll do it myself." Scott-Maxwell was dismayed when the nurse laughed and responded, "You're the kind that gets well quickly. Some who want everything done for them, just won't take themselves on at all." Need I say that I recommend being more like Florida Scott-Maxwell than the others of whom the nurse spoke?

Don't be afraid to ask to see your children from time

to time. Grown children have their own lives to lead, of course; we expect that. But sometimes they get so involved in their day-to-day activities that they forget about us. It's no bad thing to say, "Come and visit me. I'm perishing to see you and my grandchildren." Most of them are willing to come. They just need a little reminder. Besides, it shows you care whether they're there or not. Some may even think that with your busy senior citizen life, you don't have time for them anymore.

Another thing, if your children want to buy you something, let them. Maybe they think you ought to have a garage-door opener, for instance, "for safety's sake and to keep you out of the weather." Don't say, "Oh, why bother?" Or, "I can afford that myself if I want one." Instead, accept the gift and be grateful. Sometimes children need to feel they're helping their parents, perhaps to pay them back for the love lavished on them in childhood or for the grief they caused their parents. So accept the garage-door opener, or whatever is offered. It is more than a gift.

Collective Responsibilities

So much for our individual responsibilities but what might our collective responsibilities be? These could include:

• Join with others—of all age groups—wherever possible in working for the betterment of your neighborhood or your community.

• Join a church, choir, club, or senior citizen center. Be active in whatever you join.

• If there is no senior center in your community, link up with others in helping to start one. Then work to see that the center becomes an active, vital force.

• Work with others in seeing that local citizens are made aware of the condition of seniors in your community.

• Set up a support group for senior citizens who are housebound. In such a group, members are assigned to make daily calls to other members to check on their safety and well-being.

All these specific suggestions for carrying out your responsibilities, both individually and collectively, were guided by the thought that "age is an attitude."

If you decide to be old, you will be old.

If you decide to be self-dependent, and involved in life, you will remain young at heart. And yes, in body, as well, I believe.

Think of the changes that would be brought about if each of us would adopt these attitudes. Think of the effect on those persons with whom we are in association—and what about ourselves?

There are many who feel the same way, and they are the individuals who are finding the "gold" in the golden-age period of life. To sum up, our responsibility is to:

1. Care about others.

2. Be involved so that our brain power doesn't decline from lack of use.

3. Keep ourselves healthy so that we won't become a burden.

4. Be active in some kind of fulfilling role.

It's a simple formula but it promises new dimensions to your life. You will meet new friends. You will feel better. Your health will be better.

We look for magic solutions—and overlook the powerful magic we have within us—the power of changing lives, including our own, through recognizing that "We Have Responsibilities."

13

Challenges You Can Help Meet

*"Nothing is accomplished
without first being a dream."*

Will I receive my Social Security check every month for the rest of my life?

Will I have to go to a nursing home? If I do, will it be a decent place and will I be treated well there?

These are the questions I hear most often from seniors with whom I talk in Hometown America. Because of articles in newspapers and magazines, they wonder if their Social Security check will continue to arrive with regularity. For some, that money is their sole means of support; for others, it makes the difference between living spartanly or living reasonably well. On the second question, seniors look ahead and see themselves becoming the "old old" and eventually being put in a nursing home—and you know the stories that have emerged on television and in the press about this experience. Both of these areas can be problems, and that is why I say, "We have challenges."

At the moment, thanks to changes made in the Social Security law by Congress, at President Ronald Reagan's urging, Social Security seems to be safe. Yet, more and more articles are appearing in newspapers, magazines, and even on radio and television warning that the ever-increasing numbers of the 65+ population will become a burden on society. This, it is implied, will in turn create generation-gap problems. A recent article in *Washington Post National Weekly* states: "In the new America, the old are being enriched at the expense of the young, the present is being financed with tax money expropriated from the future, and one of the legacies children appear to be inheriting from their parents is a diminished standard of living." And the story goes on, quoting various political personages and citing data such as "the over age 65 population receives 51 percent of all government expenditures for social services, from pensions to education."

What prompts such articles is the projected growth of the senior citizen population. At this writing, the 65+ population represents more than 28 million Americans, or about 12 percent of the total population. However, according to *Aging America,* a report published by the U.S. Senate Special Committee on Aging, the 65+ population will swell to 35 million by the year 2000 and balloon to 64.5 million in 2030, or 21.2 percent of the overall population. Another factor creating concern is the increasing burden on wage-earners who support Social Security beneficiaries. Back in 1945, it took 50 active workers to support each Social Security recipient. In 1985, 3.3 workers carried each such pensioner; in

2030, two workers will have to bear the load. However, Congress made provisions to meet these problems when it revised Social Security in 1983, and it will doubtless do what is needed to keep this most important program solvent.

Social Security — Who Pays for It?

We hear much about the federal budget deficit these days, and somehow seniors get the blame for it. However, it should be understood that whenever reference is made that such a large percentage of the federal budget is directed toward the cost of programs for older persons, it is because Social Security expenditures are included. Yet, *Social Security is not a part of federal government expenditures. Revenue to the Social Security fund comes from contributions by employees and employers. No contributions are made by the federal government in any way whatsoever toward Social Security benefits.*

For these reasons, increasing numbers of individuals and a few politicians are questioning the Social Security system and suggesting that it's a means of taxing today's producers to provide benefits that are disproportionate to today's 65+ers. Fortunately, this is meeting with no success, according to a recent Gerontological Society of America report released at a hearing of the House Select Committee on Aging. The report states that "young people favor programs which aid today's older persons and that will eventually help them when they themselves retire. And older persons support education and community enrichment."

Some Suggestions

In view of the concerns that Social Security has created among seniors, let me offer some suggestions for improving the program. These are:

1. The Social Security Fund should be taken out of the federal budget as soon as possible. In point of fact, Congress amended the Social Security Act to provide that as of 1 October 1992 the Social Security System be a separate fund and not a part of the annual federal appropriation. *However, 1992 is not soon enough; withdrawal of the fund should come much sooner than that.*

2. Public members should be added to the system's Board of Trustees. This, too, is provided for in the Social Security revision—but should be done prior to 1992.

3. The Board of Trustees should be mandated to issue an understandable annual report and see that it is given widespread distribution.

4. Congress should pass an amendment allowing for Social Security increases to those beneficiaries whose total incomes are below the government benchmark for a minimum standard of living. Among these would be survivors of deceased Social Security recipients and the disabled. Currently the U.S. Department of Health and Human Services considers the poverty line for one person to be an income of $5,770 annually, with $1,960 more for each additional person.

I feel that when persons reach 65+ they should be assured an annual income equal to whatever is established as being at poverty level. All older persons, now and in the future, should be able to finish their remaining years with dignity and self-respect.

5. Because of the increasing trend toward automation and use of robots in mass production, a means must be found for recouping the Social Security tax monies lost by displaced workers. Compounding this trend are the periodic downturns in the economy and narrowing ratio of workers supporting Social Security beneficiaries.

Many ideas have been offered as possible solutions. Then Labor Secretary William Brock suggested in testimony before a congressional panel that the government consider scrapping the payroll tax as a way of funding Social Security. In its place, he advocated a consumption tax, such as a sales tax. (You may remember that in 1933 Dr. Francis Townsend advocated that method of financing in support of the Townsend Pension Plan.)

However, granting the need for machines displacing people, because of world competition in trade, I feel a better answer would be to consider levying Social Security taxes on robots and computers. This may sound frivolous, but I offer this idea in all seriousness. Think about it.

Ways You Can Help

These five suggestions, together with the Social Security amendments already on the books, should help make life better and more secure for today's Social Security recipients and those to come. You can help, too. Here are some ways:

• Keep informed on what's happening in this vital area of government.

• Work in concert with other senior citizens in effecting change you believe in.

• Find out the position of your congressman on senior citizen issues, including Social Security.

• Write letters expressing your views and explaining why you believe as you do.

Your time will be well spent. Adequate income is important to the attainment of a life of health, honor, and dignity at any age. It is particularly so for members of the 65+ Generation. Most seniors are dependent upon Social Security income either totally or in substantial percentage; and this is very much the case for a growing number of older women who live alone.

Congress recognized the importance of income to older persons when it enacted the Older Americans Act of 1965 and included as its first objective "an adequate income in retirement in accordance with the American standard of living." The challenge of those of us who are a part of the New Generation 65+ is to see that Social Security is protected from political attacks and that it be recognized for what it is—a contract between generations.

An Emerging Industry

Now let us turn to the matter of nursing homes and other types of care for those 65+. As stated in an earlier chapter, the individuals confined to nursing homes at any one time represent only about five percent of the older population. Others, however, may need or wish to take advantage of other services for the elderly. Indeed, as the 65+ population has increased, a new growth industry has emerged, comprising retirement communities, nursing homes, home care services, educational and recreational centers, adult day care centers, and the like.

As this industry has grown, it has naturally attracted for-profit corporations. This is particularly true with nursing homes. As Joseph Califano, Jr., secretary of the U.S. Department of Health, Education and Welfare from 1977 to 1979 states in his recent book *America's Health Care Revolution*—70 percent of the 1.5 million nursing home beds are in institutions owned and operated for profit.[1]

The fact that the nursing home business is in the multibillion dollar range and is characterized by large-scale for-profit corporations should not affect the quality of care. Yet the question remains, does large-scale operation provide for the tender loving care so vital and important in a nursing home?

Why have we seen congressional hearings being held regularly since the 1960s about the substandard, and in some instances inhuman, care in many nursing homes? In 1986, Senators John Heinz and John Glenn introduced legislation to improve the quality of life for elderly and disabled Americans who reside in nursing homes.

It has been said that nonprofit operations or for-profit corporations where the owner is on the site assure better quality care. Whether that is so is naturally debatable. I have seen good for-profit nursing homes as well as good nonprofit ones.

In his book *Unloving Care: The Nursing Home Tragedy*, Bruce C. Vladeck has concluded that for-profit nursing homes are more associated with poor quality of care in general than nonprofit homes.[2]

Personally, I feel more nonprofit operations should be a part of this growing health care industry. Why aren't there more religious groups, fraternal organizations, and service clubs spearheading such an effort in each of the communities in the United States? Many of the finest nursing homes are under the direction of religious organizations.

And what about seniors themselves? Within each community can be found 65+ers who have management skills and experience in organization, as well as others with technical knowledge in a variety of fields. Why can't subsidiary nonprofit corporations be established through senior citizen centers, which are becoming such an integral part of our communities, in conjunction with religious groups, service clubs, or fraternal organizations?

Seniors Meeting the Needs of Seniors

There are other possible approaches that I could suggest but primarily it's a matter of someone, or a group of concerned persons, spearheading such an effort. Seniors meeting the needs of seniors.

Can it be done? Not only can it be, it *is* being done. In Brooklyn, New York, there is a nonprofit corporation named GeriPare that provides minor home repairs. Since its beginning some seven years ago, the organization's staff of retirees has tackled thousands of jobs from minor plumbing leaks to replacing door locks, fixing small appliances, and performing numerous other tasks.

Undoubtedly, throughout the country, there are many similar operations involving persons 65+ providing services to others of the same age. There is no reason why such operations shouldn't be found in every U.S. community. We have a challenge as well as an opportunity to bring into being a new concept in nonprofit corporate operation.

Visualize within your community nonprofit corporations with older persons as board members and in key roles in:

Independent living housing

Nursing home or nursing homes

Home health and home care services

Adult day care centers

Child day care centers

Assisted living settings

Senior employment centers

The foregoing represent some possibilities; others would unfold with time.

An Impossible Dream?

I know that this might sound like an impossible dream. Yet look back into your life, or at life as it is or was around you. Many things that seemed impossible have become reality. Nothing is accomplished without first being a dream.

Can we meet the challenges I have outlined? I hope that at least they will stimulate some thought. From my personal experience in working with a wide spectrum of older persons for many years, and in the development of aging programs, I know the challenges can be met. Many important gains for older persons came from their own collective efforts. You can find such examples in communities throughout America.

An Afterword

---

*"Many things we call aging
are simply atrophy due to disuse."*

Isn't it strange that when we are young we give no thought to what it might be like when we become "old"? Old is always an age we have not yet reached. Not until you hit 65 and become eligible for Social Security will you subconsciously think of yourself as old.

Why should that be? As I have emphasized throughout this book, there is no set time when you become old. Never once have I met any person 65+ who considered himself old. I'm sure you'll agree that President Reagan doesn't consider himself old nor does Senator Claude Pepper. I myself, at 74, don't consider myself old.

"Continue to Plant Trees"

You'll only become old if you ignore a bit of sage advice offered by the scientist who was largely responsible for the development of research on aging by the federal government, Dr. Nathan W. Shock: "Continue to plant trees all your life expecting to see them tall and strong. Many things we call aging are simply atrophy due to disuse."

That's the philosophy I have found among so many 65+ers. They look at the 65+ period as they did those preceding it. They accept the fact that they have been blessed with an additional phase to their lives—with the opportunity to continue as they had been doing or to attempt something different. Above all, they want to keep active and in some measure contribute toward a better society.

A better society arises not only from outstanding leadership but from the basic fabric of its members—the ordinary citizens. Look back on our history from its very beginning: It was the cumulative effort of the ordinary citizen that always has made the difference.

The benefits—the values—the opportunities that we have had represent the heritage that was passed to us. It is our responsibility to preserve and pass that heritage on to those who follow.

Man's quest for fulfillment—his eternal desire to secure the blessings of liberty—is either advanced or set back by the approach of each generation for the solution of its problems.

Don't we as the New 65+ Generation have an even greater responsibility than any other younger-age group to do our part to see that the blessings that meant so much to us are passed on to those who follow us?

In my meetings with thousands of persons 65+ over more than 20 years, I have been moved by the many who are responding to the above question in so many ordinary yet inspiring ways. Some I have referred to in various chapters. All have their reasons for doing what they do while a part of the New Generation.

Consider the view of the late David Rubinoff, the eminent violinist, who for many years captivated Americans with his artistry. At 90, Mr. Rubinoff performed regularly, especially before young audiences. As his audience was captivated by his virtuosity, it also listened as he related what this country meant to him and how he was mindful that you must do what you can because time is precious. To emphasize his point, he would read a poem engraved in a watch presented to him by his friend the late Will Rogers:

> The clock of life is wound but once
> And no man has the power
> To tell just when the hands will stop,
> At late or early hour.
>
> Now is the only time we own
> Love, live, toil with a will.
> Do not wait until tomorrow,
> For the clock may then be still.

Benediction for the New 65+ Generation

May you and I, as senior citizens, always comport ourselves in such a way as to assure that passersby will say, with admiration and respect, "There goes a senior citizen" or better yet, "a seasoned citizen."

May we make our retirement period a time of self-renewal, a new plateau of life dedicated to God, our fellow man, and our communities.

Let us live a healthy life so as to set an example for other seniors, leading to increased life span for those who follow.

May we always be of good cheer, being sure to smile, give a friendly greeting to others, whether a senior citizen or not, and pass a sincere compliment when possible.

Let us make learning and growing an integral part of our retirement lives; and never stop dreaming, for dreams mean believing in the future.

Let us make good use of our experience, knowledge, and wisdom, for others as well as for ourselves.

Let us be active and stay active to the very end, remembering that, even when disabled, it is not what we have lost but what we have left that counts.

Even though we are senior citizens and part of a group, let us remain individuals and express that individualism, within the bounds of society's rules.

May we be ever creative in living our retirement lives, so as to make the last part of our lives the best part.

References

The following is a chapter-by-chapter listing of books mentioned in *The Joys of Aging*. It is presented for the benefit of readers who may wish to pursue further the thoughts expressed.

Chapter 1   Life Begins at 65

1. Walter B. Pitkin, *Life Begins at Forty* (New York: McGraw-Hill, 1933).
2. Arthur Rubinstein, *My Young Years* (New York: Knopf, 1973), 362.

Chapter 2   65+—A New Generation Profile

1. Robert N. Butler, M.D., *Why Survive? Being Old in America* (New York: Harper & Row, 1975/1985).

Chapter 3   Renewal—Not Retirement

1. Jean Hersey, *The Shape of a Year* (New York: Scribners, 1967), 181.
2. May Sarton, *The House by the Sea: A Journal* (New York: Norton, 1977), 27.
3. Jean Hersey, *The Touch of the Earth* (New York: Seabury Press, 1981), 150.

Chapter 6   Good Health Is Found in Motion

1. Norman Vincent Peale, D.D., LL.D., *The Power of Positive Thinking* (Englewood Cliffs, NJ: Prentice-Hall, 1952).
2. Hans Selye, M.D., *The Stress of Life* (New York: McGraw-Hill, 1984 Rev ed.).
3. Ronald Blythe, *The View in Winter* (New York: Harcourt Brace Jovanovich, 1979), 13.

Chapter 7   Be Alive to Stay Alive

1. Sam Levenson, *In One Era and Out the Other* (New York: Simon and Schuster, 1973), 190.
2. Norman Cousins, *Anatomy of an Illness as Perceived by the Patient* (New York: Norton, 1979).

Chapter 9   Don't Waste the Time You Have Left

1. Jean Hersey, *Gardening and Being* (New York: Continuum, 1982), 53.

Chapter 10   Act Your Age . . . Most of the Time

1. Ashley Montagu, *Growing Young* (New York: McGraw-Hill, 1981).
2. Charles Dickens, *A Christmas Carol* (First printed in London in 1843; today published in various editions and available in any public library).
3. Sarton, Ibid.

Chapter 11   You Have Power and Influence —Use Them

1. Richard Bach, *A Gift of Wings* (New York: Delacorte Press, 1974), 110.
2. Kahlil Gibran, *The Prophet* (New York: Knopf, 1923/ 1983).

Chapter 13   Challenges You Can Help Meet

1. Joseph Califano Jr., *America's Health Care Revolution* (New York: Random House, 1986).
2. Bruce C. Vladeck, *Unloving Care: The Nursing Home Tragedy* (New York: Basic Books, 1980).

MARTIN A. JANIS, a native of Toledo, Ohio, had been busily involved in the business and community life of that city until 1960. That year he was elected to the Ohio House of Representatives. In 1963, Gov. James A. Rhodes appointed him as Director of the Ohio Department of Mental Hygiene and Correction, the first layperson to hold such a position in the United States. In 1965, he established within that department, the Administration on Aging, Ohio's first official program in behalf of its older citizens. Mr. Janis served as Director of the Ohio Commission on Aging for eight years. In January 1977, the Secretary of Health, Education and Welfare, Caspar Weinberger, appointed Mr. Janis to the Advisory Council of the National Institute on Aging. In 1981, Mr. Janis headed Ohio's delegation to the White House Conference on Aging, where he served as chairman of one of the fourteen workshops of that conference. In August 1984, he received the 20th Anniversary Achievement Award of the National Association of State Units on Aging. Still very active in senior citizen activities, Mr. Janis maintains a busy speaking calendar.